Laying Something Down

poems: 1962–2007

JIM BURNS

Shoestring Press

Typeset and printed by Q3 Print Project Management Ltd,
Loughborough, Leics
(01509) 213456

Published by Shoestring Press
19 Devonshire Avenue, Beeston, Nottingham, NG9 1BS
(0115) 925 1827
www.shoestringpress.co.uk

First published 2007
© Copyright: Jim Burns
The moral right of the author has been asserted.
ISBN 13: 987 1 904886 49 5

Shoestring Press gratefully acknowledges financial assistance from
Arts Council England

ACKNOWLEDGEMENTS

The poems in this collection have been selected from the following books:

Some More Poems (R Books, Cambridge, 1966)

The Store Of Things (Phoenix Pamphlets, Manchester, 1969)

A Single Flower (Andium Press, Jersey, 1972)

Fred Engels in Woolworths (Oasis Books, London, 1975)

Playing It Cool (Galloping Dog Press, Swansea, 1976)

The Goldfish Speaks From Beyond The Grave (Salamander Imprint, London, 1976)

Aristotle's Grill (Platform Poets, Gisburn, 1979)

Notes From A Greasy Spoon (University College, Cardiff, 1980)

Internal Memorandum (Rivelin Press, Bradford, 1982)

The Real World (Purple Heather Press, Cowling, 1986)

Out Of The Past: Selected Poems 1961–1986 (Rivelin-Grapheme, Hungerford, 1987)

Poems For Tribune (Wide Skirt Press, Huddersfield, 1988)

The Gift (Redbeck Press, Bradford, 1989)

Confessions Of An Old Believer (Redbeck Press, Bradford, 1996)

As Good A Reason As Any (Redbeck Press, Bradford, 1999)

Take It Easy (Redbeck Press, Bradford, 2003)

Short Statements (Redbeck Press, Bradford, 2006)

For Joan, for being there.
"We'll always have Paris."

And for John Freeman,
good friend and honest critic.

CONTENTS

WHAT IT IS LIKE

It is like
standing in front
of a door,
and no matter
how many times
you open it
and step through
you're always
on the outside.

It is also
something akin
to a small bird,
in a cage,
looking at itself
in the mirror
and always thinking
it is dealing
with a stranger.

KITCHEN SONG

She has a way with her to make
pots and pans fall down
in homage as she passes, and

each day we lose a glass or
cup or saucer, and she
is my lady of the fragments.

THE COMPANION

One more morning, and the bus is held up
because of a crash on the road. "A car
under a lorry," someone says, and I look away,

thinking of blood and hospitals, and my wife
waiting to go down to the operating-theatre.
I glance back at the road and the ambulances,

and realise how it's all around us, like the
old woman in the doctor's last night, talking
about the "Deaths" column in the local paper.

"The biggest I've ever seen it," she said,
almost with a note of pride in her voice for
the fact that we can die in droves, "And

a lot of them young," this with contempt
because their dying at an early age
proves how weak the younger generation is.

I telephone the hospital when I reach work,
and ask how my wife is, "Oh, she hasn't been
down yet," they say, and I settle at my desk.

Going home that night we again pass the place
where the lorry hit the car. There's nothing
left to show that someone died, and probably

the people passing don't know a thing about it.
I think about my wife in hospital, waiting,
and I wonder whether she too feels lonely.

THE DIFFERENCE BETWEEN US

My father, in his younger days, had
chased pirates in the China Seas.
shelled Bolsheviks near Vladivostock,
brawled with bottles and knives
in a Mexican bar, and nearly had his
throat cut in a barber's shop
in Ireland at the time of the Troubles.
He had also been a steeplejack,
a docker, and a labourer, not to mention
one of the army of unemployed, walking
twenty miles a day in search of a job.
Towards the end of his life it happened
that we both worked in the same factory.
Those were, I suppose, his quiet years,
sweeping floors, and drinking two pints
only each Saturday lunchtime, because
his bowels wouldn't take it anymore.
He hadn't much to say, that tired old man,
when we met in the pub. He would laugh
about the time he jumped ship, or remember
what was said to him when he got drunk
and missed the sailing of the Royal Squadron.
I asked him why he'd killed Bolsheviks,
and he didn't know, it was something
that had happened long ago. The few good
times came back, the odd words spilled out
from conversations forty years before,
a sight seen, like the Grand Fleet in line
at Jutland, would come into his inner eye,
and he would lean on the bar, and quietly
look out to sea. When he died they scattered
his ashes at the crematorium. The old sailor,
who rarely spoke of anything but ships,
lying amongst the soil and grass he didn't
know. Any water would have done, the shore
at a seaside resort, or the river even,
but instead he was thrown onto a garden.
Flowers and poems. He would have laughed
at what we gave him for a funeral.

NOW'S THE TIME

Oh no, he would say,
not today,

and she, understanding,
would excuse him.

In time, today
became tomorrow, and

the next day, too.
but their love was true,

and she lived with him
until she met a man

who would, any day
or night of the week.

The problem then arose
that because he'd been

the one yesterday, he
thought she would stay.

Only if it's today,
she said.

Oh no, he said,
and let her go away.

TRAVELLING PEOPLE

Her letter said
she'd left him in
Istanbul after an
argument, both of
them expecting too
much of each other.
She'd then gone to
Tel-Aviv and I could
reach her there
with news of what
had happened in the
town while she'd
been away. And Oh
yes, he'd been
smoking hashish a
lot of the time and
that hadn't helped,
but she was wiser
now and had laughed
about it since.
She was living with
an Australian girl,
in a flat owned by
a Jewish professor,
who was also
a part-time painter,
but didn't know where
she'd go next, so
I wasn't to worry
if I didn't hear
from her for some time,
she'd probably be
travelling around,
you know, seeing people,
and doing things.

THE INFLUENCE

I wish that women in the
garden would stand still.

The trees, sky, fence,
rooftops across the field,

are perfect for painting,
piled up on top of each

other, in slabs of colour,
and all without movement,

but she insists on bobbing
up and down by the window.

Later, she'll be inside,
breaking up the tidiness

of the house, pushing the
clock back an inch, sliding

a chair forward, and leaving
papers scattered all around.

This poem, too, has been
disturbed. It could have

become a cool description
of the garden, but instead

it has turned out to be
yet another portrait of her.

THE COLOUR OF …

When she stands near
the window, you can see
it's auburn, but I
tell her this, and she
shakes her head, laughs,
and says I'm wrong.
You should marry
a woman like that,
and then spend your life
following her around,
watching for that moment
when the light shines through.

THE BOHEMIAN GIRL

She was once fucked
by a famous poet, and
forever after was
accepted as an authority
on the arts. "One has
to feel it," she'd say,
and we'd sit silent,
knowing that she spoke
from experience.

NEVER TAKE ANYTHING FOR GRANTED

A girl called Tania
in a town near Stafford,
and a girl in a white coat
in front of Lord & Taylor's.
Both surprisingly have
places in my thoughts,
drifting ones, perhaps,
but places to stumble on
when I least expect it.
Last week, Tania turned up
on the telephone, in the
voice of a girl from Blackpool.
Tomorrow, walking through
the streets, it could be
I'll come across a shop
called Lord & Taylor's, with
a girl in a white coat
waiting out front for me.
Never take anything
for granted. What you
can't see is all around you.
Ask General Custer, he knows.

THE FANTASTIC SCREEN

The women in those 1920s films.
How sweet the heroines look,
with long, white dresses,
pale, innocent faces, and soft
sad eyes. And they're always
so small and helpless!
I watch them clasp their hands
as they wander across the screen.
see them swoon in terror
as the sniggering villains
sidle in to carry them off.
And then the temptresses turn up
to distract the heroes.
They're slinky, sensuous, and bring
memories of faded old photographs
of sex scenes. Hands gripping hips,
legs entwined around necks,
wet lips bending towards breasts.
Ah, the women in those flickering films.
Tie that boring virgin to the rails!
Let that train thunder down the track!
Call my mysterious mistress back.

REPORT FROM THE HOME FRONT

She broke the chalks
in half, a piece
for each of them,
and split the board
down the middle.
Giving them both exactly
the same would save trouble,
she said, but damn-it,
they drew different pictures,
and then started fighting
about which was best.

THE WAR AT SEVEN

When I was seven
I sat on the wall
at the end of the street,
watching the convoys.
Trucks full of troops,
armoured cars, trailers,
guns, even tanks, with
the surface of the road
cracking beneath them.
We walked into town
to scrounge chewing-gum
and peanuts from the
Americans. "Got any gum,
chum?" we asked, and
had our hands filled
with tins and packets.
On the way home the Italian
prisoners were wandering
along in groups. No-one
bothered about them, they
wore denims, with P.O.W.
on the back, and were
friendly. Quite a few
later married English girls.
That summer my brother
had a map in the house, with
flags pinned to it, showing
where the Allied armies were.
I didn't worry, war was a
G.I. handing out peanuts,
or an Italian playing football
with us. It was also
John Wayne battling in Bataan
on Saturday night, and a
friend's father coming home
on leave with spurs on his
boots. And I remember
a boy from my class standing
in a corner of the playground

one morning, with tears
in his eyes. He wouldn't
tell us why he was crying,
but the same day I noticed
that the curtains in his house
were all closed, and I thought
it odd for five o'clock
on a warm, summer afternoon.

A GOOD DAY

Hell, who wants to write poems
when there's pea-soup waiting?

    A good day for both, really,
    the wind cold, and the rain

    drizzling down.

Come to think of it, a good day
for making love, too.

What decides the preference?
    (poems, pea-soup, or an afternoon
    in bed with a willing woman)
Age, maybe, or an appreciation
of what's involved – the keeping
up of strength, etc.

OK, then, to settle it,

    write the poem,
    eat the soup,
    and go to bed,

the order determined by a desire
to end with a bang.

A WAY OF LOOKING AT THINGS

My son can see a man's face
in the remains of the chicken!
Figures appear on the walls,
and (strange this) there are
cities in the fire.
Last night I saw him looking
at me. No laughter on his face.
No words spoken. Just a long
thoughtful look that I
pretended not to notice.

NIGHT SEQUENCE

What she left behind

A nice way to go,
he thought,

as she went out
for the night,

not leaving a kiss,
or a smile even,

just a nod, and
the words, "Be good,"

and the thought
that she should.

2. The need

He stubs his toe
against a chair,
and swears. "Why
the hell did she
leave it there?"
She didn't, it's
in the usual place,
but her absence
makes him that way,
angry because
she's not home
when needed,
even if it is
only to be blamed.

3. Reading a book about Bunker Hill

She comes in,
and sees him
sitting hunched
over the dying
embers.
"Fire," she
shouts, and he
jumps up,
blazing away
at the white
of her eyes.

THE CRACK

She took the fragments
and stuck them together
again and it looked
all right except that
there was a line straight
across the middle and
somehow she couldn't
get it to hold without
this line showing no matter
how she tried. Oh well,
he said, that's how it
goes, you break it once
and it's never going
to be the same. Yes,
she said, you bastard.

WHEELS

My son is drawing, turning wheels,
building up a series of circles,
spreading slowly over the paper,
black lines, circling and circling.

Looking at them, I'm reminded
of an old pithead, the wires circling,
the wheels turning and turning.

And my thoughts drift thirty years,
to the Autumn I played on the beach,
beneath the mine, throwing stones,
watching the evening mist come down.

"Hear now, home before seven,"
my grandmother said, "Or you might see
something you won't much like,"

meaning the ghosts of dead miners,
gone forty years before. A hundred men
buried there, and the broken wheels
creaking in the wind, wires trailing.

They're half a mile out, under the sea,"
an old man told me, "But some people
say they've seen them at the pithead,

With their helmets and lamps and all.
Not that I think there's any truth in it,
though years ago a lad along our way
came home crying one night for no reason.

That was just after it happened.
There were streets of women wearing black,
and a lot of fatherless children.

They soon closed the shaft down,
reckoned it wasn't safe anymore,
but you can't close down a town's grief.
One little girl pined away and died."

In the cemetery he takes me to
a small, worn stone: "Desdimina Yates,
who fell asleep, April 3rd, 1909."

The thick lines blend with the thin,
the wheels wind and spin on the paper.
"Who fell asleep, April 3rd, 1909,"
turns gently in my mind.

THE CONDITION OF THE WORKING-CLASS IN BRITAIN IN 1974

I am day-dreaming again about Engels'
Irish factory-girls, Mary and Lizzie Burns,
and I reconstruct the line
which shows that one of them had a son
who took his mother's name, and so,
somewhere, there's a link with the old German.
He was much better than that prig, Marx.
I can see Fred Engels riding to hounds
with the Cheshire Hunt, enjoying it,
and in any case it was good training
for the days when he'd lead the cavalry
of the revolutionary army. And in my mind,
I also see Lizzie showing her work-torn hands
to poor Tussy, and asking what the middle-class men
who hung around Fred's house
wanted from the workers. Bodies for the barricades?
Fred was all right, he enjoyed life,
and at least looked after a couple of the poor.
And all this makes me think
of the last time I was in London, a place
with more middle-class pinks per mile than any other
in the world, and a pretty young girl
wanted me to pay fifty pence for a copy of
a Marxist-Leninist publication, designed to show
the workers the way, and lead to close relations
between the true left in all walks of life.
I asked her if she'd sleep with me in the interests
of the overthrow of the class system,
and she screamed and called a policeman.

THE COLUMN

The hum of the heavy lorries,
revving up and down the loading
bay of the ferry warehouse,
disturbs me, and makes me think
of the hum of army vehicles.
I recall three-ton trucks
with bored teenagers at their
wheels, the huddled figures in
the rain at the head of the column,
the crackling transmitter
with its occasional American voice
calling for "Red Dog Charlie,"
the Sergeant-Major striding along,
rapping on the mudguards with his
cane, and telling us to "Put those
bloody cigarettees out." Mud and
rain and two trucks piled in
a ditch, one driver bleeding from
a cut on his forehead. No-one
badly hurt, thank God, and I radio
to the rear of the column
and tell them to prepare to start
up again. The leading tail-light
slides off into the dark, and we
follow, slowly bumping in and out
of potholes. I notice a house
in the distance, and ask the driver
where he thinks we are. He shrugs
and swears and wrenches the wheel
to one side. "Search me,"
he says, and in the light from
the dashboard I can see the lines
on his face. We halt, and I
climb out and stamp my feet. A pale
glow is working its way up the sky,
and the rain has stopped. I rub
my itching eyes and pull at the
sticky collar of my shirt. "The
C.O. wanted to take a leak," an
officer grumbles, stumbling past me,
down the column, and I grin.
The engines start to hum again.

MY SAD STORY

I never did get to be
General Custer.
It was always me who ran
the fastest
in retreat. Three strides
ahead of the rest, and first
through the hole in the hedge,
I tell you it was shameful
the way
I wouldn't stop and fight.
So, the kids decided I couldn't
ever be
Custer or Crazy Horse or even
Sitting Bull, hanging around
the village,
cooking up big medicine.
Instead, they made me
the obscure trumpeter
who was sent to the fort
to ask for help.
That way
they filled all
the necessary roles,
and kept me out of the fight
as well.
The only thing was
I never did have the chance
to make it to that fort.
I had to sit on the hill overlooking
the battle,
watching them kill each other off,
and then I'd check in late
with the old story that
I'd taken a wrong turning.
No glorious Custer,
no wild Crazy Horse,
no foxy Sitting Bull,
and not even a part of the sweating
relief force

arriving too late!
Just the old lonesome trumpeter
riding around
passing on messages
about death and disaster.
That's my sad story.

FRAGMENT OF A DISORDERED EDUCATION

I was educated in an outside lavatory,
reading yesterday's paper, torn into
handy squares to fit the family seats.
The war came and went, I crapped
and read on, getting only half of the
stories, pondering about the rest,
and wondering who had wiped their bum
on last week's inspiring speech.
Peace and prospects next.
     I was older,
got interested in the politics of the
Daily Mirror. Clement Attlee was my
hero, I saved the sheet with his photo
until the last and used it gently. It was
sad to have to flush him down the drain,
but it had to be done. The 1940s slid
by, and mother hinted that it might be
nice to have a proper toilet roll.
     Father,
full of memories of the Depression, said
nothing, and busily tore up the Daily
Herald. The economic crisis of 1952,
can anyone tell me what it was all about?
I never was sure, the next sheet on the
hook had racing results. And Korea,
what were they fighting for? The reports
I read ended half-way down the page.
     We
stumbled into 1954. Mother had her way,
Father hated to see good papers wasted,
and took to covering the kitchen-floor
with them. A new era in my education
dawned. I learned to read the latest news
upside down from six feet away.
     It didn't
seem to make it any better, though.

LOOKING FOR A CIGARETTE

"Are you in a hotel room in Detroit
looking for a cigarette?"
        Charles Bukowski

Half of my life has been spent in hotel rooms,
looking for cigarettes. And it's usually
the early hours of the morning, the bottle
is empty, and the radio playing a tune
that brings back memories of other hotels,
and emptied bottles, and crushed cigarettes.
If I were in a movie a faded blonde
would walk the floor in a creased negligee,
and a neon sign flash its message
at regular intervals outside the window.
But the only movie is in my mind,
and it's yet another journey into the past.
A blonde does walk the floor, and a sign
flashes on and off, but when I open my eyes
I can see faded wallpaper, and an empty bottle,
and a crumpled cigarette packet.

THE STIMULANTS

He shows me a new poem, written,
he says, on Mozart and marijuana.

I show him a new poem, written,
I say, on be-bop and bitterness.

We look at each other's new poems,
and drink glasses of cool lager.

We wonder what it would be like
to write new poems on nothing?

AT THE GRASSROOTS

Coffee-bars are only for intellectuals,
and workers use cafes, so I stride
into the local one at lunchtime,
and order my cup-of-tea and three
sausage-rolls. As I'm eating, I feel
a nudge in the middle of my back,
and overjoyed at this friendly approach
by a member of the proletariat, turn to
look at a weatherbeaten face.
"How did we get on?" the mouth mumbles,
between bites at a ham sandwich,
and I reply, "The bastards twisted us,"
jabbing with my forefinger. "Bloody
knew it," he says, "Bloody knew it,"
and I tell him, "They had us taped
right from the word go." He snarls,
"It was bloody obvious before we even
started," and I shout, "We'll get our
own back," and he assures me, "Too true
we bloody will," as he lifts his custard
from the counter. "Yes," I say, "We'll
pack the next meetings and vote them out."
"Vote who out?" he asks, and I say,
"The committee," and he looks at me as if
I'm mad. "The union," I add, and he says,
"Bugger the union, I was talking about
the cup-tie," and I ask, "But what about
the union?" and he says, "Jesus, are you
another of those bloody Commies?

DEATH

I used to imagine it would be an old man
who'd come walking in one night in a
long, black cape, and he'd flourish it,
and quickly fold me to him, and that
would be that. And once I even glimpsed
a lean, dark-eyed female, like someone
out of a silent movie, all slinky
and evil, and I cowered in a corner as she
closed in and blotted out the screen.
Then I had a vision of a blonde angel, with
wings which would embrace me as I slide into
a sweet and gentle sleep.
          But recently, I've
started to think about the middle-aged women
who serve me in shops, and a moment later
I can't recall a single thing about them,
or the man who accepts my bus-fare,
and the girl who hands me the drinks
I know will take me through the barrier,
and when I finish them I realise there
isn't any barrier, and even if one existed
there'd be nothing on the other side of it.

GETTING ALONG

All right, she leaves, and you think,
to hell with her, I'll get along,
but as you wander through the house
you can still hear her song.
You open the wardrobe and find the
coat she left behind, you look into
a drawer, and there are some ear-rings.
Memories dangle in your mind.
You find a hairpin on the floor,
beside the bed, you open your eyes
in the morning, and there's not a crease
in the pillow where she used to lay
her head. You make a simple breakfast,
you sing a familiar song. You hear it
echoing through the empty rooms,
and you think you'll get along.

THE PERSONAL TOUCH

In dancing I dislike
precision, the tidiness
of pre-arranged patterns.
The tune should determine
the way the feet move,
that, and the mood, making
the measure something
personal. How can a dance
have meaning if it is just
a sequence of steps
designed to please a crowd?

IN THE LIBRARY

The book I pick up is called Unrest 1930,
The Rebel Poets Anthology, and all the poets
are marching together with clenched fists,
falling in behind the Red Flag,
and beckoning to the watching workers.
The future is somewhere up ahead of them,
and how can they know of Spain,
and the Communist slaughter of the Anarchists,
or 1939 and the Nazi-Soviet Pact,
and Hungary in 1956, and the well-fed years
and immigrant-baiting affluent workers?
They can't, of course, because no-one knows
the future, and few would want to believe it
if they did. And so, they parade, shouting
slogans, "basking in the warm love
of proletarian hearts," and praising Stalin.
Even hobos are welcome, the days of "decadent
individualism," and "disruptive elements"
have not yet dawned, and the red ranks
advance across the pages, comrades all,
"bards with rebel tongues," "in the service
of mankind," "defiant, exultant, victorious,"
as they disappear down the years, growing
smaller, voices fading to a broken whisper.

WINTER, 1947

A season of heavy snow,
piled high in the streets.
So high I had to climb through it
to get to school. No cars,
no-one could afford them then,
and the factories closed through strikes
or fuel shortages. Men peering out
from frosted windows. There
seemed to be queues for everything,
the butcher had no meat to sell,
we pooled our coupons for sweets,
and found we couldn't buy them anyway.

I was eleven, the sharp days
were always heady and exciting,
and the town had sixteen cinemas.
My sister's boy-friend gave me money,
I spent my nights with Hollywood,
Lana Turner looked so good.
At home, the radio rang out
all the changes. I heard
my first Woody Herman record,
and thought Sinatra weak and sloppy.
The snow fell steadily,
we swept it away from the door,
my mother gossiped with the neighbours,
and father read the Picture Post.

In Europe, the refugees crowded into
dreary camps, the shattered cities
were full of stray dogs,
there was talk of some sort
of iron curtain. I saw it all
as a newsreel, and mixed it in
with Flash Gordon. My world
was covered with a warm, white blanket,
and then I awoke one morning,
and found that everything was grey.

THE OLD REVOLUTIONARY SPEAKS

We began with demands for freedom,
and finished by filling in forms.
After all, what else was there to do?
The bourgeoisie had all been shot,
or at least the three of them
willing to admit to being of that class.
Everyone else wore mufflers and caps,
a little new, perhaps, not frayed
at the edges, but still mufflers and caps,
and none of us wanted to make the mistake
of eliminating a genuine worker.
And the army had been properly purged,
forty corporals made captains,
and forty captains made corporals.
We thus dealt with privilege
by turning things upside down.
We levelled all the hills,
and filled in all the hollows, so that no-one
lived higher or lower than anyone else,
and we abolished every differential
of money and creed and culture.
All one had to do to obtain one's rights,
was fill in a form, and present it
at the right place, at the right time,
and, of course, in the right way.
After all, what else was there to do?
It is only by filling in forms
that one deals with demands for freedom.

WAITING FOR McALMON

It's raining outside,
and we sit in the bar
waiting for the afternoon
to end. The place
is dead. Two pensioners
huddled in a corner
with glasses of cheap wine,
a workman looking into
his beer, the barmaid
bored with wiping bottles.
The book lies on the table,
between us. We glance
at it. Bob comes in,
his face pale from
last night's booze. He
needs a drink, he says,
wiping the rain off his
shoulders. We order again.
The silence is depressing.
"No work today, Bob?"
and he shakes his head.
"I think there's something
happening later,"
he says, and picks up the
book. A grim fairly tale.
"We could move on, see
what's further down," he
suggests, and we shrug,
thinking of the wet streets,
the pedestrians huddled
under the awnings, the
dripping policeman directing
traffic through the town.
"Something's sure to happen,"
falls on the empty chair.
We cut through the years,
picking up fragments
from forgotten magazines,
wishing we'd been there.

THE BUSINESS

I look through an anthology,
noting names and dates. Hart Crane
died when he was thirty-three,
Frank O'Hara when he was forty.
Others lived until they were sixty,
or seventy, a few even until eighty.
Weldon Kees went out when he was
forty-one, Mina Loy (1882-1966)
believed in carrying on. God,
it's an unpredictable business

A WOMAN OF SOME EDUCATION

There are secrets in these places,
and possibly legends. The shabby lady
who pulls her possessions around
in a wheeled shopping-basket, stands
in the half-empty afternoon bar,
and moves her arms and legs
like a puppet, and mutters some
unintelligible language. "In a
concentration camp," the man across
murmurs from behind his white wine.
"Latvian or Pole or something," and
he lapses into silence. A figure
cuts into my view of the wired woman,
a man with a beard who, they say,
flew fighters in the war, and lost
his mind when he crashed in the Arctic.
He drifts on, and the woman continues
her nervous dance. The wine drinker
lifts his glass to his lips, and they
open again. "A woman of some education,"
he says, and then sips slowly
as she struts and jerks in time
to some terrifying distant music.

THE GOLDFISH SPEAKS FROM BEYOND THE GRAVE

Twelve years swimming from
one side of that tank to the other,
bumping my nose against the glass,
turning around, flicking a fin,
and bumping it again. Christ, if they
only knew how boring it all was.
The same food dropped in each day,
the water changed once a week.
They couldn't even let me live in
darkness, so insistent were they
about knowing what I was doing.
And when I was dying, and wanted to
lie at the bottom of the tank,
they rapped on the glass, and pushed
their squirming faces against it.
The horror is that there is no horror,
but there is certainly despair,
and I knew what that was all about.
Well, it's finished at last,
and I've been buried in the garden.
A perfect end for an English fish,
helping to push up the weeds, so that
the family will have something else
to worry about each Sunday morning.

COMMUNIQUE TO A CHILD

First of all, you must not complain.
The bomb that blew off your left leg,
and tore away one of your eyes,
was placed by some of our volunteers
to obtain maximum psychological effect
in the struggle to achieve our demands.
It was not our intention to maim
or kill anyone, and we regret the death
of your mother. However, you must
accept that there are no innocents
in a situation such as this.
So, adjust to your present condition,
and do not condemn us. As you
limp into the future your one eye
will enable you to see things clearly,
and you will evaluate the event
with the wisdom of age. You will
begin to understand why it happened.
Only an adult can possibly know this,
and apply reason to the suffering.

The roofs of Vienna are wet again tonight,
and the old apartments leak scratchy sounds
of half-forgotten sad songs. Below me
an ageing veteran of the Spanish Civil War
coughs out his life in an alcoholic haze.
If you go to the corner of Beckumerstrasse,
and say the right words, you'll maybe meet
a foreign agent, or a high-heeled prostitute,
and either can initiate you into secret moves
or mysterious positions. A black car hurtles
through the deserted alleys, someone struggles
in the back seat. The policeman looking
the other way will not live to see morning,
the car will leave the city and head towards
an unknown destination. The gramophone
grinds down, the fire flickers fitfully.
Outside the window a soft whistle signals
"The Internationale." I don't know what to say,
but the ghosts have ways of making me talk.

THE SKY IS CRYING

Rain nearly all day,
and the view across the fields
depresses me. Heavy clouds,
wet grass, trees losing
their leaves in the Autumn
wind. Along the side of the dock
the derricks spill water
continuously, the petrol tanks
are bleak against the sky.
The bus sprays the rain over
the pavement, sodden flags
hang limply from ships' masts.
And through the misted window
I can almost see other towns.
Munster, twenty years ago,
the warm, back-room of a bar,
the subdued voices, your head
resting lightly on my shoulder.
Or the railway station in Soest,
the damp smell, the weary
passengers in the waiting-room,
the distant shouts of the Dutch
soldiers across the tracks,
loading tanks onto a train.
Your hair glistening with
raindrops. Tears in your eyes.
Strange how the rain
makes me think of you.
Lying in bed, late at night,
listening to it hiss under
car wheels on the road, or
drip from eaves, I recall
a hotel room in Arnsberg,
nights with you in my arms,
whispered words and soft hands,
the blanket kicked onto the
floor, and then pulled back
again when the sweat cooled.
And always, it seems, the rain

lashing against the windows,
or dripping endlessly
into my dreams, a constant
reminder of a day caught out
in the country without coats,
two or three miles from the
village. We found an old shed,
and went into it and made
love on the dirt floor, your
damp hair clinging to my face
as I pressed against you,
and, of course, those whispered
words falling from our lips
as the rain splashed into
the barrel outside the hut.
Beyond the river the lamps
glimmer, the rain running down
the window slices through them,
distorting the rays. Pinpricks
of light flick through the
night. The rain falls steadily.

EASTER IN STOCKPORT

I am sitting in a comfortable high-rise flat
over-looking the industrial wasteland of Stockport
(Wasteland! This is going to be very poetic!)
and the past comes quietly creeping in on me
like a smooth grey smog from the factories.
Easter in New York, April in Paris,
why do they bring this Spring feeling
when I know I don't want to be anywhere else?
Irene is in the kitchen, cooking breakfast.
Isn't it romantic? And last night we made love
for the second time. You would be surprised
at what happens in those high-rise flats.
But here they come again. Old poems, old songs,
memories flooding in as the lock-gates open.
I see her face before me, half-hidden behind
a boiled egg and the morning paper. My mood
is swimming in a coffee cup. The radio is
pumping out another old song, but I can't place it,
and some lines from a poem slip through my mind
like shadowy ships sliding into the Frisco fog
in a flickering Forties mystery movie.
We ought to be high on a windy hill, the sky
is up above the roof. The smoke from a cigarette
curls between us. A photograph of a French poet,
ash-heavy cigarette dangling from his lips,
snaps up on the screen. Easter in New York.
"The girl with paper roses on her straw hat.
They sing through eternity who sing like that."
The Belle of New York? Old films, old poems,
old songs, memories. Irene rustles the paper,
clinks a tea-spoon against the sugar-bowl.
The weak sun starts to climb high into a sky
of shifting clouds. Noises drift up from the street.
Easter eases in like a slowly melting chocolate egg.

FRIENDS

Friends, who chase their girlfriends into busy streets
after arguments in restaurants, and are then arrested
for non-payment of the bill, and attempting to assault
a passer-by who thought he'd better intervene.

Friends, who stagger around drunkenly, and mumble weird
stories of outrageous debts incurred in Hertfordshire,
after which it was never the same again with their wives
or their writing, and they don't know which is worse.

Friends, who make mad arrangements to meet other friends
in strange places, and then find a dozen large policemen
waiting for them with dogs that sniff out certain scents,
and land them all in court afraid of their conspiracies.

Friends, who leave their wives or husbands or lovers or
both, and take to sitting alone in darkened rooms watching
quiz shows or cartoons on silent TVs, while they pick at
endless packets of potato crisps that are always dry.

Friends, who sleep with sleazy saxophone players, and soon
pass on the marks of it to their husbands, and come crying
when they beat time on their heads while the children
huddle at the top of the stairs and repeat the obscenities.

Friends, dear friends, whose lives are a part of my own,
and whose exploits and escapades turn me out of bed
at the most outrageous hours, why should I complain about
your behaviour? After all, I'm a friend in deed.

LONG DISTANCE

The soft voice trickles
over the telephone.
"I'm all screwed up again,
four hours tonight,
talking over our problems,
why I've done this,
and why I don't do that.
It's no way to live, is it?
I've got to get out,
or I'm sure I'll go mad."

200 miles away, I stand
in the call box,
watching the rain sliding
down the glass panels,
and listening to
the torrent of sad words.
I'm about to mutter
some meaningless phrases
when the line clicks,
and then goes dead.

I'm undecided.
Should I dial again?
Do I want a reconnection
to those complaints
I can do nothing about?
Distance dulls the impact
of most disturbances.
"It can't be all that bad,"
I tell myself,
and replace the receiver.

SCRAPPLE FROM THE APPLE

East Side, West Side,
all around the town,
the hipsters said, "Bird Lives,"
even wrote it down

on the subway walls,
in the canyons of steel,
as they hustled for a living,
a fix for their next meal.

Dewey Square to 52nd Street,
black circles spinning around;
the hipsters are all dead now,
Bird lives in his sound.

THE WORLD IN THE MORNING

Sun through the trees,
dew-damp grass glinting,
wire-mesh fence making
patterns on the
cool stone steps.
It's good to get up,
breathe clear air,
listen to the birds,
and smell the new day's
sweetness. A butterfly
flutters across the garden,
pauses, and drifts on.
Bees hover over flowers,
children's voices cry out
from the fields by the river.
For a moment my mind,
and the world, stop moving.

ULLA IN AUTUMN

Autumn is on us again,
and I think of you.
In the park the leaves
are piled high for burning,
the bare black branches
are stark against the sky.
I take the top road, recalling
how I once held your hand
as we walked by the river,
the gold and brown leaves
clinging to our shoes, the
morning mist moistening your
hair and leaving my cheek wet
as I gently brushed my lips
against your face. Across
the valley a tiny figure
moves through the trees.
I stand on the slope, wishing
you were coming to meet me.

ALL THOSE YEARS AGO

I remember a bookshop
in London, and an American
saying to me, "Frank O'Hara got killed,"
and I replied, "It's a bad week,
Bud Powell died, too."
And yet I've just read some O'Hara poems,
and yesterday I was given a Powell record.
The words are written down,
the music goes round and round.

THOSE OLD JAZZ PHOTOGRAPHS

Hey, look at them there, hair
slicked down on either side
of their heads, and holding
their horns as if they were
going to hurl them at us any
moment. Wow, what music they
must have played, way back
in the Jazz Decade. I can
almost hear it now, that tight
rhythm, and those hot licks,
and the smooth-toned singers
slipping sweetly through "Tea
for Two" and "Exactly Like You."
I wonder where they are now?
America must be full of old men,
living in rooms with greasy suits
hung behind the doors, and waiting
for someone to ask them if they
ever bought Beiderbecke a beer.

THE OBSERVATION

Three days without her,
and then the way
a girl's hair rests on
the nape of her neck
reminds me of what I'm missing.

It's always the simplest things
that hit hardest.
A few loose strands of hair
are enough to bring
the old desires back again.

SNAPSHOTS FROM MAY, 1926
(The General Strike took place in Britain in May, 1926)

Three pretty girls in gay hats
sit around a garden table,
feeding cream-cakes to a pekinese.

Several women in shabby shawls
cluster at a street corner,
children clinging to their skirts.

Two fresh-faced youths in sweaters
smile bravely from a bus,
a policeman perched behind them.

A dozen sullen men in worn suits
stand, hands in pockets,
staring at an armoured car.

Snapshots from fifty years ago,
the smooth surfaces cracking,
and the bitterness seeping through.

GOODBYE

And that last afternoon,
lying in bed,
listening to the rain
on the window.

Three long days later
I thought of you,
high above the Atlantic,
lost in a cloud.

THE DAYS OF WINE AND ROSES

Poems to the pink and black
of silk and lace, poems written
for forgotten girls in rooms
littered with tumbled skirts,
poems on absinthe, poems about
love and death and sin, and poems
around the moon and the night.
The pages reek with the scent
of them, the delicate lines
transmit their simple messages,
the occasional words in French
and Latin display decadence
or religion, or perhaps both.
"Life was easier then, and so
was art," though the poets died
or despaired quickly enough
from a surfeit of the two.
But the poems still live,
they survive the sentiment,
or even thrive because of it.
An old man once shyly told me
he knew no lovelier lines than,
"Ah, love, the sweet Spring blossoms cling
To many a broken wind-tossed bough,
And young birds among branches sing
That mutely hung till now,"
and that they had sustained him
through the autumn deaths of dreams,
and the winters of war.
"Much of their poetry was personal
and rather superficial,"
and yet it is no mean thing
to have written a few lines
that can forever touch the heart.

THE PERFORMANCE

We sit in the bar,
listening to the musicians
talking about chords
and choruses, and he
suddenly says, "Well, it's
done, I've left her."
The conversation across the
room carries on,
a trombonist is discussed
and dismissed,
drinks downed, and
cigarettes passed around.
"How was it?" I ask,
and he replies, "Awful,
she cried and cursed,
and finally ran out
of the house, and went
into town, and told everyone
what I'd said."

There is a pause,
another voice horns in,
a half-sung song
explains a point.
"It's the way it goes,"
I murmur, wondering
what else there is to say,
and he nods.
The musicians pitch
their opinions collectively,
the sound is discordant.
We drink, and silently
exchange glances.
His baffled eyes
are those of a man
who has lost his place
in the score,
and is desperately trying
to find it again.

THE POINT

One walked into a stream of fast cars,
and another stepped from a high bridge.
They were maybe among the best.
Some I knew died in bars with the drink
that brought out the wistful in them,
and some died gracefully in smart suits
bought with loose money earned at work
they hated. One sat in front of the fire
and said it didn't matter anymore,
and one said that it mattered, but he
was tired of carrying all the worries.
And the worst was the one who succeeded,
and then spent all his time telling us
how easy it was. He'd missed the point.

MOON DREAMS

The waves burst onto the beach,
and lovely Linda Darnell
hurried down to meet me
by the light of the full moon.
Hollywood, you really were to blame.
Whole generations of us
sat mesmerised as the bright stars
danced across the breakers,
and the foot-high bosoms
heaved in time to the hazy music.
Those fragments of melody,
and the richly-tinted screens,
made dreamers of us all,
and condemned our divorced wives
before we'd even met them.

BONAPARTE'S RETREAT

Christ, all that snow!
Miles and miles of it
everywhere you looked,
and the silly bitch
I had with me said she
liked it, everything
seemed so pure and clean.
She was only facing
her front, of course,
and the fur hood stopped
her seeing the strangers
menacing our flanks.
And she thought that
glancing back would bring
bad luck, and that's
why she never saw the
trail of blood marking
the route we'd taken.
She said she loved snow,
it levelled everything,
made it neat and tidy,
but I knew it would be
the death of us, it was
so damned hard to push
our feet through,
and if you went down
it covered you at once.
So, there we were, lost,
things coming apart,
and she chattered about
how nice it all was,
and the snow just kept on
falling and falling.

HERE I GO AGAIN
"What's the matter with me, especially
on Saturday afternoon? It seems that there's
a park nearby and people in it."
   Frank O'Hara

There's nothing the matter with me,
except that you're not around. Oh, Christ,
those thoughts. Warm afternoons,
green parks, tall trees, and always you.
Everytime I see a kid on a swing
I get happy and lightheaded. And it's
no way to be at my age. If you
hadn't walked into my life I'd still be
spending the afternoons squinting at sunlight
through dusty bar-room windows. Instead,
I'm picking up blades of grass and looking
thoughtful. A blade of grass is a blade . . . .
Now tell me something wonderful.
This is just like swinging in space.
My heart is in my mouth again,
and Frank O'Hara's poems in my pocket.

THE UNEMPLOYED NIPPLE

I am standing in line at the employment exchange,
waiting to sign to say I haven't worked this week,
when I notice that the girl behind the counter
isn't wearing a bra, and the dark stain of a nipple
shows through her thin blouse each time she leans forward
to hand a form to one of my companions in idleness.
She is clearly unaware of the effect she is having
as the hungry eyes focus on her well-shaped breasts,
and the shaking hands scribble crooked signatures.
She is a pretty girl, and it seems a pity her nipple
should be unemployed. It also seems a pity that I
am unemployed. Perhaps her nipple and I could get
together, and so solve the problem of unemployment?
Maybe I've come up with a solution to a major social evil
in one inspired flash of my erotic imagination?
The only question, as the old socialists said,
who would be the exploiter, and who the exploited?

THE GRAND TOUR

Coming down from Newcastle on a Sunday afternoon,
the train shunting up the line and back,
stopping at endless tiny stations, and we start
talking to Ormond S.Culp, M.D., and his wife,
from Rochester, Minnesota, and travelling,
they hope, to Liverpool, to pick up the rest of their
party. Two days in Edinburgh, three in London,
and then to Amsterdam and Paris. "We always promised
ourselves we'd do Europe," Mrs Culp says, and here
they are, stranded at Blackburn, eating Saturday's
curled-up cornbeef sandwiches, and sipping watery
coffee from paper cups. One wonders if Byron and
Shelley missed something when they went to Italy or
Greece? Perhaps that funeral pyre would have been
better on Blackpool beach? Maybe Byron should have
died eating sausage-rolls on Carlisle station?
Possibly Ormond S.Culp, M.D., had the right idea when
he looked over the industrial landscape of the North,
and said he'd never seen anything like it.

CHANGE

Don't blame your parents
for what they didn't do,
think about what you haven't
done yourself. You want
the grants and subsidies,
and you want to rebel.
It doesn't work that way.
You can't be in control
and still be a revolutionary,
the driving seat is always
square. You can't be the
resident poet and paint the
town red. You're either with
them, or against them. You
can't have it both ways.
Don't blame the elderly,
some of them at least tried
a General Strike. What have
you done? Don't look for the
easy way. There isn't one.
Don't let them make your bed
for you. Rumpling the blankets
won't alter anything. Get
rid of the bed and sleep
on the floor. It's uncomfortable,
but it's the only way. Nothing
worthwhile comes easy. Live
by yourself or with a few others,
and state your own terms. Work
at it. It's the only way.
Think about what you haven't
done yourself. Change

THE MELODY

The girl in the photography is naked,
back towards me, head to one side
so I can see the profile of her face.
Her body reminds me of a cello,
billowing out where her buttocks
meet the chair on which she is sitting.
I want to reach around her,
feel the swell of her breasts,
move my hands over them, and bring
music to her lips, but she is
poised in an absolute stillness.
There are no movements. No sounds.
The melody exists only in my mind.

HAVING A WONDERFUL TIME

The card arrives from two thousand miles away.
"Having a wonderful time," it says, but not,
"Wish you were here." She's happy with someone
else on a distant island, why should she ever
want me there? An old conceit deceives me
if I imagine that she does. And I don't
even know if I want her here, although I know
I want her. The sun slices through the dusty
bar-room windows. That last drink did the trick,
and I'm detached again, and not unhappy.
I think of the sun shining down on an island,
a tall, slim girl strolls along a sandy beach.
I lift my drink to my lips, and swallow the
bright liquid. Flecks of light dance through
the dregs in the bottom of the glass.
The waves bubble and burst along the shore.

WAVING

It seems that children wave
whenever they notice a train.
From playgrounds, fields,
estates of similar houses,
their hands flutter in greeting,
and farewell. There is a train,
with people on it, and they
must be going somewhere exciting.
That's how I saw it as a child.
And now, years later, on a train,
going nowhere I want to be,
I wave back to the children,
and envy them their optimism.

THE CHANGE

England at seven
on a Saturday evening
looks toy-like,
the tiny churches
spiring the fields
and villages, the
country pubs holding
light in windows,
canals and rivers
reflecting it.
Around Crewe, the train
hits rain and mist,
and the towns
change, the stones
of building blacken,
the people hurry
through the streets.

FOR AN OLD COMRADE

I thought that you
would always be there,
and that when I went back,
and walked through the streets,
I'd hear your voice
call my name.

And I imagined
that I would never forget
which pub to find you in,
and that we could drink,
and talk about jazz
and books and socialism.

I hoped that somehow
we'd share a store of memories,
and that we would laugh
about the times we'd known,
and wonder together
about friends who were gone.

And then the letter arrived
to say that you had died.
These are the days
when such news comes too often,
and all that is solid
melts into air.

POEM FOR A NEW HOUSE

Take it easy,
settle in slowly,
let the walls
grow in their own way
around you,
let the floors adjust
to your feet,
the ceilings
to your height,
the bath
to the shape of your body.
Be comfortable,
don't rush around
the place
and make it nervous.
Most of all.
be happy.
The house will hear you
and return the favour.

THE NEED

To have it near you,
and not touch it,
is a kind of discipline.
You can think about it,
say it doesn't matter,
or perhaps say it does,
decide on a reason,
or not decide at all.
Then you can sleep.
When you wake up
you'll be glad,
but it will be there,
and everything will start
all over again.

LOVE IN VAIN

Sun sinking behind the hills,
ice-cubes clinking in the glass,
radio murmuring softly,
"It's only human for anyone
to want to be in love,
but who wants to be in love in vain?"
The summer Sunday afternoon
has slipped by, evening crawls
across the fields to meet me.
"You sit and wonder why anyone
as wonderful as she
should cause you such misery and pain."
The gin hazes my thoughts,
but you're still in them.
I want to know where you are,
and what you are doing,
and why we're not together?
"I thought that I would be in heaven,
but I'm only up a tree,
'cos it's just my luck to be in love in vain."
Dusk settles in,
a cool breeze touches the leaves,
shadows and questions haunt me.

PHILOSOPHY

I am drinking in London
on a bright November day,
and someone asks about
the pretty French philosopher
I once knew.

I look out at the leaves
drifting in the square,
and think of Edith Piaf.
It seems a lifetime away,
and I could colour it
with cafes and Sartre
and that sort of existence,
but I have made a choice
to see things as they were,
and the truth of it was
she thought little
of Continental concerns,
and we walked along
the banks of an English river,
and not by the side of the Seine.
But the red and gold
of the falling leaves
makes me nostalgic again.

An old craving creeps in,
a thin taste of bitterness
cutting through the alcohol.
The question is repeated
across the noise of the pub,
and I shrug, and reply,
"Everything has to end,"
and my friend laughs,
and says, "Well, at least
she left you philosophical."

LA VIE DE SURREALISME

It is Saturday morning,
and I am strolling back from the bakery,
the sweet smell of fresh bread in my nostrils.

Walking towards me is a young priest,
owlish eyes set above tightly-pursed lips,
his air one of knowing what the world is about.

As he passes he smiles at me.
Who am I to be smiled at by a priest
when the sun is shining down on everyone?

I hit him with my French stick.
"Oh," he shouts, and scurries along the street,
his black cassock clutching at his ankles.

Bread is scattered across the pavement,
and the sparrows are hopping in anticipation.
How will I explain all this at home?

THE SIMPLE THINGS ARE HARDEST

"Would that someone would start Meditation places of silence, so
silent you couldn't help but hear the sound of your page."
                            Lorine Niedecker to Cid Corman

1.
The horse walks slowly
through the trees,
there are hens in the garden.

My friends might laugh
at words like those,
the simplicity of them,

instead of the usual
confusion of the streets.
But I wish I could

get beyond the bright lights,
and see the simple things
as you saw them.

2.
Noises everywhere:
damned neighbours, dogs,
radios, children, motorbikes.

I watch the sun go down,
draw the curtains,
and pick up a book.

"No better poetry than the quiet,"
unless it's the sound
I hear from the page.

WEEKEND CASES

"It's funny," I said,
"to wait on the platform,
watching the women
getting off the trains
with their weekend cases.
I wonder if they're all
having affairs, and what
their husbands do
until they get back?"
She was standing there,
clutching her small case,
and she smiled wryly
as she listened to me,
"Weekend cases," she said,
"that's what we carry,
and it's what we are."

HAPPINESS

Happiness is like a disease.
It takes hold somewhere in the mind,
and spreads. You find yourself
doing uncontrollable things, such as
singing or dancing or making love.
What an affliction! You can't concentrate
on the way the world is falling apart,
you don't notice how it needs changing.
Instead, you retreat to quiet places,
and forget to call for revolution.
Occasionally, you are aware
that the disease has you in its grip.
It's like cancer or alcoholism,
and you fight a losing battle against it,
unless, of course, someone comes up
with a cure for your condition.
People are always glad to attempt that,
and see it as their duty to do so.
They feed you confusion, anger, sadness,
and a stream of other medicines
designed to restore you to normality.
If you're lucky you recover, and become
like everyone else. If you're unlucky,
you totally succumb. Happiness takes over.
People shake their heads wisely.
"He wouldn't be warned," they say,
"After all, it's like cigarettes or drink,
moderation is the best policy.
You can't be happy all the time
without it having an effect on you."

THE BENEFITS

My former father-in-law,
like many men of his generation,
had seen a thing or two.

Behind German lines in 1940,
a village square, the defiant ones
tied up and bayoneted.

A view from a weaving truck
as a Stuka dive-bombed it down
into a ditch of screaming men.

The dreary beaches at Dunkirk,
the drab lines of tired khaki,
the grey ships standing offshore.

The Stuka left him partially deaf,
enough to cut him out of the everyday,
to escape bickering and complaints,

though, curiously, I often noticed
that asked quietly in a noisy pub,
he understood, and stated his choice.

Now, in rooms of the ambitious,
with the demanding, or the shrill,
and among the politically vicious,

I began to appreciate the benefits
of having seen a thing or two,
and of an occasional deafness.

OUR CHURCH

"The church is really quite nice,
lots of weddings but very few funerals."

A couple married, and from them
a couple of children.
It needs a couple of people out
to maintain an obvious balance,
you might think, but things
are not quite that simple.
We prefer a pleasant neighbourhood,
and try not to disturb anyone,
so we keep hearses to a minimum.
It is something of a nuisance,
deciding how to dispose of bodies,
but we manage somehow.
As soon as it's dark
we wheel them to the graveyard,
and put them under the soil.
Everyone pretends it doesn't happen.
"Seen John lately?" someone says,
and their friends look surprised,
and ask, "John who?"
or quickly change the subject
to engagements and births.
Of course, we do stage a funeral
every now and then,
just to keep death in mind,
but we always handle it with style,
and not much weeping,
and no-one takes photographs
as they're fond of doing
at weddings and christenings.
Yes, we like to have a lively church,
and if the children ask about
the white stones in the graveyard,
we smile, and tell them
to wait until they're older
for the answer to that one.

A MODEL SCENE

The handsome young officer
is sweeping the pretty girl
across the ballroom floor.
Other couples are poised
around them, pirouetting
in a swirl of many colours.

The young officer will never
know what it is like
to be lifted from his horse
by a long, polished lance
placed pointedly in his chest
with skill and precision.

He will never lose a leg,
so will continue to dance,
and both his arms will remain
to keep the girl from falling,
as he looks into her eyes,
and swings her gaily around.

Here, in this glass case,
nothing will ever change.
It will always be the warm night
before the famous battle,
and no-one will need to know
what happened after that.

DEAR JACK

I am sitting in the launderette,
Saturday morning,
listening to the ladies
talking about this and that.
The copies of your letters to Carolyn
came today,
and I keep glancing through them.
All that to-ing and fro-ing
in the world,
all that sadness and anxiety.
You should have stayed
with what you understood, Jack,
small-town stuff,
mill walls and the ghosts of workmen,
pool-room banter and football games.

You would have loved it here just now,
bright sunlight promise,
easy words with nothing underneath,
the familiarity of the ordinary.
I watch the big blonde
sliding her black underwear
into the machine.
Glimpses of secret pleasures,
quick smiles,
warm fumblings in half-lit bedrooms.

And lunchtime pubs on a day like this,
the men with racing papers,
winding down from the week's work.
Ah Jack, what went wrong?
Did we all get too smart,
sending Spengler through the post,
pretending we knew what was happening?
The West will decline in its own way,
and without our help.
But somewhere, there's a bar,
and two drinks on it,
and two men leaning and laughing,
with all the time that's needed
to catch that moment
when everything seems perfect.

65

ACADEMIC PORTRAIT

She sits at the dinner-table,
and talks about her career,
what Elizabeth Anscombe
once said to her in Oxford,
what Freddy Ayer thought
of her thesis on Gilbert Ryle.
Her left-hand holds a cigarette,
and is bent back over her
left-shoulder. Her right hand
rests on her left-wrist,
but occasionally swings forward
to accent a particular point.
She is confident,
and can converse easily
in English, French, or German.
And she knows that in her study
is an almost-completed review
for a prestigious publication
read in all the right places.

Her guests admire her,
and sympathise when she
makes a semi-humorous complaint
about the traumas of teaching
philosophy to middle-aged students
who somehow think that life
can tell you as much as books.
And they understand her preference
for a post in a university,
if only such things
were easy to come by anymore.
The room has darkened
as the talk around the table
has moved from this topic to that.
Outside, bright lamps
throw light on other houses,
She glances at the window,
and, realising the world is there,
gets up to close the curtains.

YOUR TUESDAY NIGHT ENTERTAINMENT ON TV

Did you watch the war on TV?
At work next day
they talk about it as if,
planned and prepared for,
it is a football tournament,
the only difference being
that the ball explodes when kicked,
and men never get up again
when they collide with death.
Expert commentators
interject their opinions,
the most exciting scenes are re-run
for the benefit of those
who, gardening, or in the pub,
missed the day's results,
and the famous man in the street
even gets to have his say
about the faults of management.
It is all a game,
best watched with a can of beer,
a sandwich, a packet of crisps,
and the wife and kids
agog with excitement, too.
Tracer bullets stream
from ship to shore and back,
smoke billows high,
a plane explodes in mid-air,
and a bandaged and grimacing player
moves across the screen.
And every twenty minutes or so,
holidays and expensive cars
are advertised with flair,
and pretty girls, half-dressed,
pour shampoo on their hair.
And then the match is resumed,
but what a pity it is
that an extra touch of reality
can't be added,
like a close-up of burning flesh,
or the shrill sound
of a dying man screaming.

A PHILOSOPHY OF HISTORY

The target for tonight is Magdeburg.
I am about to release
the first missile.
It is a very old city,
as I recall reading
when I was at University.
I was a Humanities student
before I joined the Armed Forces.
I studied philosophy and history,
and wrote a dissertation
on the Thirty Years War.
In those days, it took a Prince,
and thousands of soldiers,
more than a month
to storm the walls of Magdeburg
and slaughter its inhabitants.
Now, I and my small team
will manage as much
in a matter of minutes.
It gives one a sense
of continuity with the past
to be in this position.
If there are any libraries
left in our own country
when we emerge from the bunker,
I may go back to studying history.
It would be interesting
to know more about Magdeburg.

TODAY OR TOMORROW

When you politely ask for it today,
they say. "Tomorrow will be a better day."

And when tomorrow comes, they say,
"Ah, but it's not tomorrow, it's today."

So you go on, slowly making your way,
waiting for tomorrow to follow today,

until you give up and quietly pass away,
and that's never tomorrow, it's today.

CLASS OF 1952

He stops me on the bus-station,
and asks for the price of a cup-of-tea
for an old school friend.
I give him 50p, he asks for 20p more.
The price of a cup-of-tea has risen,
and is, perhaps, nearer that
of a glass of bitter. But, shaking
from a hangover myself, who am I
to tell him how to live his life?
We exchange a few words,
and then he shuffles away
in the opposite direction to the cafe.
I think of that bright class of thirty,
and wonder what happened to the rest?
One was early dead, I know,
going out in the way we thought best,
a quick heart attack when making love.
Another is in a wheelchair,
and has nothing to walk on anymore,
while a third is serving life for murder.
The others? Some successes, I suppose,
a solicitor, schoolteacher, shopkeeper,
several civil servants, with tidy houses,
gardens, families, and cars,
though not all escaping divorce.
But somehow I can't relate to them,
and the failed and doomed and dying
are the ones I understand best of all.
"Does it worry you"
I recall asking a friend
when he was waiting to be punished
for some infraction of the rules,
and he replied, "No, I always think
it'll all be over in another few minutes,"
and that eternal optimism appeals,
like the 70p for the cup-of-tea
that, he said, would help set him up
for the rest of the day.

A CONTEMPORARY LOVE STORY

"This isn't right," she said,
as they rutted on the tangled bed
in the cheap hotel. "Oh, God,"
he cried, "your husband, my wife,
think of what we're doing," and
they gasped and pushed their hips
at each other. "Ah," she shouted,
and he sobbed as her firm legs
wrapped around his buttocks.
"Oh," he moaned, and gripped her
shoulders. "It's wrong, it's wrong,"
she muttered, and he said, "I know,"
and they slowly began to start
their movements all over again.

THE OTHER WOMAN

We kiss on a windy corner,
he walks away to meet his wife.
I take a taxi to the University,
a departmental meeting, and sit,
thinking of our morning in bed.
The warm room lulls my senses,
voices slide in and out of time,
a note rustles along the table,
a spoon clinks on a coffee cup.
I drift in a scent of bedclothes,
and wonder about his wife,
what they're doing together.
Someone opens a window slightly,
a breeze disturbs my papers.
I float into the distance,
we kiss on a windy corner.

PICTURES FROM AN EXHIBITION

The Thirties are on show,
neatly packaged, as if to tell us
they're now just history.

But among the exhibits
something is missing,
and it begins to bother me.

Finally, I find what I want,
tucked away in a corner,
a display about the Depression.

Photographs of bleak towns,
and even bleaker people,
in Scotland, Wales, Lancashire.

I stroll on through the gallery,
look at the bright objects,
and recognise the distance.

The decade wasn't hard for all,
that's what we're being told,
and I know it's true,

but it was only in the section
where lean faces looked grim
that I somehow felt at home.

With this thought in my mind
I leave, and catch a train
that quckly takes me North.

ON THE CLOSURE OF THE STRICT AND PARTICULAR CHAPEL IN PRESTON

It was founded by people
who were strict and particular,
No drinking, no games on Sunday,
and the first week's wages
of a hard working life
donated happily to the church.
The chapel itself plain and clean,
white window-sills, pumiced step,
and inside, a room where baptism
by total immersion took place.
When the elders of the church died
they did so "steadfast in the faith."
The minister was paid a pittance,
and eked out a frugal existence.

But the congregation was small,
and as the years passed got smaller,
so that, like death, there was
an inevitability about closure.
Most had left for a better place
where the rewards of cleanliness
could be claimed from a grateful God.
And in the vale of tears these days
it seems that not too many are strict,
and even less all that particular.
I pass down the street each day,
and notice that the once-white woodwork
is streaked with cracks and dirt,
and the step is turning grey.

SEE NAPLES AND DIE?

No-one dies in Naples anymore,
other than the normal quota of Neapolitans
from natural and unnatural causes.
The visitors quite cheerfully come and go
(some even talk of Michelangelo)
and though the water may not be safe to drink,
there's always wine, and assorted pills
for hangovers and excesses of Italian food.

It's true that, a century and more ago,
various Englishmen, and the women too,
went down with the plague or the pox,
and someone wrote to unsettle the stay-at-homes
by suggesting that the deaths were due
to having seen Naples in the morning light.
But the past, we're told, is a foreign country,
and they do things differently there.

Nowadays, Naples is another sanitised trip,
but as you descend on London, look at what's below,
see the sprawling maze of the suburbs,
think of the problems at every turning,
recall the regular chatter of routine news,
taste the slice of toast each morning.
And remember that people die, as a doctor said,
from want of what a few poems might provide.

FACE TO FACE

I can't talk too much about it.
I can't let the words spill over
in the way I want them to, like
a waterfall, all dancing light.

I have to keep them locked inside,
the ones I really want to say.
I'm afraid of how you'll hear them,
of where the tumbling water goes.

I listen to your flowing voice,
know the sounds, not the meaning.
Inside I'm a raging torrent.
My calm surface covers confusion.

BEAU BRUMMELL

who, in his madness,
arranged the furniture

in his cheap lodgings
to look like that

of some scene of his
former triumphs,

and announced the entry
of the imaginary guests

until, at last, he
reached his own name,

and collapsed, crying,
in despair.

The gesture was empty
without the others

to reflect its impact,
the defiance nothing

in the shattered mirror
of his memories.

He had perfected himself,
it was his only art,

and as his mind gave way
the glass ran out.

CHINA KITCHEN

And the Oriental girl
asks what you want.
"I've seen you before,"
she says with a smile,
"You're an old China Hand,"
and you get nostalgic,
and hear the thunder rolling
from across the bay.

"Yes, an old China Hand,"
you reply, "But this
is my last time here,"
and she laughs at that,
and you feel yourself
sinking forever into
a sea of white flowers,
and her hair is black.

Then she names the price,
and you pay her,
and go out slowly,
thinking that you'll never
see her face again,
but you hear her soft voice
mockingly call,
"You're an old China Hand."

PLACE

I sit propped against the pillows
in the hotel bedroom, reading poetry.
She stands by the window, looking out
at the seagulls, sand, and rain.
It is not long since we made love,
our mood is still heavy with it.
Faint noises creep in from other rooms,
a trickle of laughter, sound of music.
There is nowhere to go on such a day.
There is nowhere else I want to be.

77

A SUNDAY KIND OF LOVE

"What are we doing here?"
said the man with glasses to the woman in blue,
as they stepped from the hotel doorway
into the thin, Sunday morning drizzle.
"Here I am, two hundred miles from my home,
and here you are, wondering how to explain
why you've been out all night."

The damp streets were almost deserted,
church bells chimed in the distance,
an occasional car slid past,
and the man with glasses and the woman in blue
held hands as they crossed the road.

"It can't go on like this," she said,
and he replied, "I know," and they turned
their heads away as she thought she recognised
a neighbour's daughter. "My God," she said,
"if it was her, and she saw us,
he'll hear all about it by tomorrow."
"Don't worry," he murmured, "don't worry."

Later that day, the woman in blue
sat with her husband and children, and chattered
about the old school-friend she'd met,
and how she'd been too tipsy to drive home.
The man with glasses caught a train.

CONFESSIONS OF AN OLD BELIEVER

"Wisdom comes by disillusionment"
    Santayana

It was 1945.
I was nine years old
and full of enthusiasm
for our gallant Russian allies.
SECOND FRONT NOW was scrawled
in foot-high letters
on the air-raid shelter in the street,
and along a gable wall
were the words, SUPPORT THE CP.
On VE Day everyone hung out Union Jacks,
apart from my Uncle Stan
who had a Hammer & Sickle
outside his bedroom window.

In the nearby cinema
they played the National Anthem
at the end of each programme,
but followed it quickly
with The Cossack Patrol,
and I knew which was more exciting
as visions of snow
and The People's Army
came swirling into my mind.
After all, wasn't it Stalin himself
who'd concocted the recipe
for Uncle Joe's Mint Balls,
and so guaranteed to keep us all aglow?

There was something in the air.
I saw Harry Pollitt plain
and watched Willie Gallacher on a street corner
speaking to a small crowd.
He was flush-faced and fat
and wore a shabby, belted raincoat.
The local Labour Club
was at the end of our street,

79

and it wasn't what I really wanted,
but I collected numbers
outside the Polling Station.
They gave me a hot-pot supper
and five shillings,
and I knew I'd been compromised.

I held on until 1948,
Masaryk fell from a window in Prague,
there were rumblings around Berlin.
By 1950 it was almost over.
Iron Curtain, spies, Korea, strikes,
everything had gone badly wrong.
I sat on the edge of the pavement,
my feet in the gutter,
watching the dirty rain water
trickling over my scuffed shoes,
and sneaking longing looks
at the well-spoken, uniformed girls
on their way to the Convent School.

I knew things could never be the same,
and in any case the Party
would not accept my discovery of be-bop,
that decadent American music.
The air-raid shelters
had long since disappeared,
and the words on the gable-wall
were faded and almost unreadable.
I tore up my commitment,
tossed the pieces in the air,
and watched them scatter in the cold wind.

ON STRIKE WITH GRETA GARBO

It is a hot summer's day,
and I am helping to picket the local Town Hall.
"Listen," I say to the shop steward,
"three hours of this, and I'm
off to watch Greta Garbo in *Camille*."
Just then the Chief of Police, known to us all
as God, drives past in his limousine.
We give him a friendly wave and ten minutes later
several of his men turn up to tell us
which picketing rules we're breaking.
Greta Garbo still looms large in my thoughts,
and I am imagining the cool interior
of a beautiful French chateau,
when a firm hand steers me to one side
and a couple of delivery vans pass through the gate.
The shop steward scowls at me.
"You could have stopped those vans," he says,
"if you hadn't been daydreaming."
I look at the policeman standing in front of me,
and at the shop steward standing behind me,
and I know how Greta Garbo felt
when she said she wanted to be left alone.

PARIS IN THE SPRING

"Paris has changed," she said,
but it looked the same to me.
A line of riot police pushed us
along the rue de Rivoli, and I
could see the sunlight glinting
on their helmets and shields.

"I tell you, it's changed," she said,
but it sounded the same to me.
The horns of the police vans
blared up and down the boulevards,
as people yelled with fear,
and cars hurtled around corners.

"Oh, but it's changed," she said,
but it felt the same to me.
A truncheon jabbed at my stomach,
and someone kicked my shins
as I suddenly back-pedalled,
beginning to feel my age.

"Do you think we've changed?" she said,
and I'd got to admit we had.
My legs wouldn't move fast enough,
but my breathing was quick and jagged.
And I knew the French for "bastards,"
but I didn't dare to shout it.

STANDING FAST

"It's a lost cause," he said.
"Maybe," I replied," but somehow,
I think I'd rather be out here,
lost and damned, than inside
with those who never had a cause
to fight about and lose."

PEACE IN OUR TIME

Who were they,
those young soldiers?
I'm standing in shirt-sleeves
with four or five others,
behind us the recovery vehicle,
beyond that the workshops.

And I can't recall their names.
I know they were members
of the same platoon,
and that they all got home safely.
There was a war, Suez,
but we weren't called to it.

So, what happened to them,
what kind of lives did they make
for themselves on their return,
following that couple of years
of barracks and bar-rooms,
and wet and miserable manoeuvres?

Everyone, when they left,
said they'd write and stay in touch,
but no-one ever did. What for?
They'd only the ordinary in common.
They went home, got drunk, found jobs,
were married, and had kids.

But I miss everybody,
and recall that day we had the photo
taken by a German workman.
Arms around each other's shoulders,
thumbs up signs, and smiles.
I'm the only one looking serious.

Perhaps I knew that fifty years later
I'd sit and wonder about the rest,
if they're still alive and where,
and what they're doing now.
Perhaps I knew that soldiering
would be my only time at peace.

PHILOSOPHY WITH GEORGE

I am sitting in the barber's chair,
and he tells me about his trip to Alaska.
"The ice-floes are melting," he says,
as my grey hair falls to the floor.
"Another fifty years or so and the land
will have disappeared beneath the sea."
Another five years or so, and he
won't need to clip my hair so close,
it will mostly have gone anyway.

Everything comes and goes, I think,
ice-floes, hair, the barber, and me.
"What can we do about it?" he asks,
pausing to pick up a keen-bladed razor.
I hold myself still as he shaves my neck,
and reflect on the nature of his question.
He finishes, and I pay him. "The future
doesn't look at all inviting," he says,
and then, "I hope to see you again."

BEHIND THE MASK

I am not given to using gentle words.
Usually, I assume the role of jester
to a court slowly going mad
on its own illusions. They like me
that way. I dance, strut, sing,
am even a little bawdy if it fits,
and I can occasionally make them cry
with reminders of their lost youth.
It is all done in short doses, of course,
and with a certain casualness
that disguises my lapses into contempt.
People rarely take me seriously,
and I am glad. But sometimes,
lying awake in the dismal early hours,
I look at your head on my pillow,
and I take off my bitter mask
to speak a few gentle, serious words.
You are asleep and do not hear them,
but they have been spoken,
and only for you.

JOHN'S STORY

I used to watch these American films,
you know, and they always had a hero
who'd come in and say, "I'm just going
to take a shower, honey," and he'd do
just that, and later he'd open the fridge
and take out a large carton of orange-juice
or milk, and pour himself a glass full,
and I told myself that when I grew up
I'd do the same, so I do, every night
I tell my wife, "I'm just going to take
a shower, honey", and later I have milk,
or a tall glass of cool orange-juice,
and I think about the two-up, two-down
I grew up in, and the lack of a bath,
or a shower, and the fridge we didn't have,
the orange-juice you couldn't get,
and the souring milk in a pan of water,
and I think, if anyone tells you about
the good old days in England, you can
tell them from me to shove it up their ass.

MANCHESTER MOOD

Walking down Market Street,
rubbish around my feet,
paint-sprayed slogans everywhere,
and a ghetto-blaster blaring
from its owner's arms,
I think of Engels many years ago
on this same street,
and wonder what he imagined
the future would be like.

SHUT DOWN

I walk the streets of Pittsburgh,
and see America without its heart.
The closed-down steelworks
and smokeless chimneys,
the unemployed ageing in unpainted houses.
Life does go on, the centre is clean,
the streets are full of cars,
and the shops sell almost everything.
But something is missing,
and the feeling isn't right.
I search in vain for the warmth
that comes from work both cursed and shared.

IT TAKES A WORRIED MAN

Suddenly, all my friends
are involved with trivial pursuits.
They watch soap-operas on TV,
play quiz games in pubs,
and spend hours telling jokes.
I never know what to say to them
when we meet. They look askance at me,
and make sarcastic comments
about people taking themselves seriously.
There is a silence between us,
disrupted only by the sounds
of music and fruit-machines,
by the climax of yet another joke.
One more emotion has died.
I shuffle uneasily,
and wonder whether I
should have been in at the kill?

THE STOIC

"I don't trust happiness," he said,
and you couldn't blame him.
Twenty years faithful to one woman,
and then he found out
she'd slept with all his friends.
And a job since he left school
that suddenly ended when the boss
ran off with everyone's money.
Never any steady work after that.
He took to propping up the bar
most nights and weekends,
not saying much to anyone,
and hardly looking beyond the next day,
until the doctor told him
he had only a year or so to live.
That was the first time I saw him
with a smile on his face.

TO END ALL WARS
    My mother's story

He was in the Territorials,
and in 1914 they called him up
and sent him to France.
I only saw him once after that,
when he came home on leave
for a couple of days,
and I looked at him in his
uniform, and I said, "No,
I don't like you in that."
And then he went back to France.

I was in the schoolyard one day,
and a boy ran up, and shouted,
"Janet Wilson, the Germans
have killed your Dad,"
so I flew at him and hit him,
and he said, "It's true,
I've seen your mother, and she's
crying in the Post Office."
And that's how I found out
how my father died in 1915.

SISYPHUS AT THE DSS

Each morning I take the tray of papers
and begin to work my way through it.
The complaints are always the same,
not enough money, too much suffering,
and my responses adopt that pattern.
I never apportion blame, it's not my job,
but instead, I fashion replies
which explain about the shortage of funds,
and other, more-deserving cases.
Eight hours later, I clear my desk,
take my coat, and close the door.
Overnight, someone fills the tray again,
ready for me to start on in the morning.

FASCINATING RHYTHM, 1953

Dublin, Sunday morning, September,
and I wander through the quiet streets,
trying to keep myself awake
after an all-night crossing of the Irish Sea.
I can still feel the rhythm
as the ship hit the rise and fall of the waves,
still hear the urgent voices
talking about now-forgotten records.

And later the same day, a theatre in the city,
the excitement as Zoot Sims
strolls to the microphone, raises his tenor,
and starts the first solo of the concert.
Stan Kenton smiling, all tiredness gone,
no thought of the long journey home.
Nothing but the rhythm,
and the rise and fall of music in my memory.

AUTUMN IN NEW YORK

I wonder what I thought I'd find in New York?
Old communists speaking in Union Square,
Jack Kerouac on Macdougal Street,
Bird at the Jazz Corner of the world,
Franz Kline sitting in the Cedar Street Tavern?

Forty years of books and music and paintings
drifting around in my head,
I knew the place so well
a stranger asked me for directions,
and I told him which turnings to take.

But nothing remained of what I'd gone to see.
Wanting time to stand still,
forgetting all the lessons of history,
I think I expected to find myself in the city,
and instead met someone who was lost.

RADIO NIGHTS

Looking back, I see a radio,
the dial lit with names and numbers,
the arrow tuned to a foreign station,
Hilversum, Cologne, Stockholm, Paris.

I kept my ear close to the speaker,
careful not to wake anyone else
in that small, terraced house,
tucked away in a Northern backstreet.

"God knows what you do half the night,"
my mother grumbled, and my father
said it was time I took things seriously,
stopped wasting my life on books and jazz.

During the day I was half-dazed
from lack of sleep, and shuffled through
a routine job. No-one else I met
had ever heard of the names I mentioned.

But they were known to me: Wardell Gray,
Dexter Gordon, Fats Navaro, Al Haig,
Sonny Stitt, Charlie Parker, Kenny Dorham.
Heroes of the midnight hour.

And now, fifty years later, I still
hear them. I switch the tuner in my head
to a distant station, adjust the volume,
and let the music cut through the dark.

PARENTS

"Go and see if he's coming."
my mother would say, and I'd run
to the end of the street,
and look along the main road
for the small figure
swaying slightly as he walked.

Still, drunk or sober,
I never disliked my father,
and always thought that the poet
who said that your parents
make a mess of you
was talking a poet's nonsense.

Who wouldn't have been glad
to see that tired old man,
and any mess I later became
was completely of my own making.
That was something I learned
from both of my parents.

CHINESE COMPLAINT

The room is tidy again.
No coats thrown over chairs,
no pens and pencils scattered
across the record cabinet,
or cluttering up the fireplace.
I can even find the daily paper,
and now my life is so ordered
that I have time for everything.
I straighten the curtains,
see neatness all around me,
and look forward to it
disappearing with your return.

THE STIMULUS

Looking back,
it strikes me as funny,
all those poems
about a lady
who didn't give a damn
whether a poem
should be written or not.
But it was, perhaps,
the indifference
that aroused the desire.

SNACK BAR
          after a painting by Edward Burra

He's slicing meat
behind the counter,
she's eating meat
in front of it.

He's got a smile
on his fat face,
she's got a mouthful
of his neat meat.

The red of her lips
moistens the meat,
his lips are wet
as he watches her eat.

He offers her bread,
she waves it away,
then says, "Hey, Pete,
let's eat more meat."

ON THE PAGE

Looking through a magazine,
I come across a poem
alone on a page,
whiteness surrounding it.

The poem is about
a white dress.
Everything in it is simple,
and it touches the heart.

Elsewhere, deep theories
run in solid blocks
from margin to margin,
as if afraid of an open space.

I turn again to the poem,
and the words delight me.
I see how the poet
has used that whiteness.

THE GRAVE FACE

You should start to feel worried
when the human race puts on its grave face.
Flags fly, anthems strike up,
and, given the right circumstances,
people will quickly begin to die.
They may already have died, of course,
when the grave face is on display,
though the music will be slightly different,
and the flags a little lower.
So, always beware of the grave face.
When it's around
you're either in your grave, or soon will be.

QUEER

God knows how he survived that small town.
The only "queer" around, or obviously so,
swishing along the main street Saturday night,
the bus drivers honking their horns
and people whistling and shouting.

Or the cinema on a dull Sunday evening,
the sudden roar that raised the roof
as he wandered down the aisle,
his seat tipped up when he tried to sit,
gobs of spit rubbed into his hair from behind.

The beatings, too. The bus station late Friday,
when the young drunks were on their way home
and needed some activity to satisfy them
for not having picked up any girls.
It made them feel good to make him cry.

I never knew why he stuck it out,
unless it was some kind of perverse courage.
I'd have left long ago, had it been me,
but I was safe enough and simply turned away
when I saw him being pushed and prodded.

And I hear he's dead now and I'm ashamed.
He stayed to defy convention and I quit the town,
bored with the poverty of its imagination.
In his own queer way he went out undefeated.
I decided to write about it somewhere else.

LIFE IS A DAY LIKE THIS

It is January 2nd, a Saturday,
and I awake with a feeling of anticipation.
There is so much ahead,
now that the world is returning to normality,
and I catch a train into the city
in order to renew my role
as a stroller of its boulevards.
The bookshops are almost empty at this hour,
and I browse comfortably,
no anxious elbows in my ribs,
no Christmas coffee-table tomes
blocking my access to the volumes I desire.
I buy a book, a collection of essays,
and look forward to reading about Pataphysics,
or the 1935 Congress in Paris
at which a variety of famous writers
failed, as usual, to form a popular front.
Well, as Pasternak said of poetry,
"It will always be too quiet a thing
to discuss in meetings."

I stroll on, thinking of Marlene Dietrich,
who I will accompany in Weimar Germany
into the early hours of the following morning,
and I enter a small record-shop
to be greeted by the sound of a saxophone
riding high and handsome
over cymbal splash and throbbing bass.
I chat with the man behind the counter
about the sensitivity of Zoot Sims
and the strangeness of Don Byas in Barcelona.
The day is producing so many marvels.
Soon, I relax in a bookshop
and talk of Manchester and James Joyce,
the juxtaposition not as strange as it seems.
The dead may be just that,
but they are around us all the same,
and it is far better to pass
in the full glory of some passion,

saying yes and yes and yes,
than to fade and wither dismally with age.

Later, I am delighted to discover
that The London Review of Books
and The New York Review of Books
are available once again,
and that the weekly magazines are on schedule,
with what is monthly in its rightful place.
The glass is clearing slowly,
and there are little hints
that weird-looking animals might suddenly appear,
and suggestions of galleries
where something new will be revealed.
I stand on a street corner,
watching the umbrellas jostling for space,
but I think of a 1940s song,
and I can see the sun when it's raining.
There is a quiet bar not far away
where I can glance through the papers,
and reflect on the effects of the wine.
Who knows, an offhand turning of a page
could bring something unforeseen.

A LIFE AND DEATH THING

I watch the funeral
of one of my neighbours,
his friends parading
the coffin around the Green.
Neat-suited men,
with rows of medals,
slowly walking past
and into the Church.

After they're inside,
the young undertakers
lounge against the hearse,
sucking ice lollipops,
and eyeing the women
in their summer dresses
as they collect children
from the nearby school.

THE STREET
"The street – the only valid field of experience"
        Andre Breton

A lazy summer afternoon reminds me.
The street of terraced houses,
sky a bright blue above the roofs.
Shouts, curses, and cries,
someone always seemed to be arguing.
The occasional drunk
wavering along the pavement,
voice raised in a tuneless song,
a crowd of kids imitating him.
Tarmac bubbles and smelly grids.
Sips of lemonade, if you were lucky,
or an apple passed around.
Too hot to play football,
too bored to want to play cricket.
A languid feeling that life
would surely remain this way,
warm and ordinary.
On certain days now, I close my eyes,
and think of faces I'll never forget.

THE SMILE

When I was a boy
she was pointed out to me
as the town whore.
I know there must have been
more than just her,
but that fat, ungainly woman
captured my imagination.
What would she not do?
Huddled behind the bike-shed,
we traded tales of schoolboys
sampling her for half-a-crown.
One was said to have been seen
disappearing into her house
in the late afternoon,
and we wondered if he
had ever come out again?

She was always a mystery to me
until, on a summer evening,
wandering alone by the river,
I pushed through the long grass,
and came upon her in the act,
skirt pulled up to her waist,
and with a thrusting man,
pants around his ankles,
sprawled on top of her.
I paused, and as I did,
she looked over his shoulder,
and gave me a little smile.
I stared, then fled,
and for almost sixty years
have wondered about that smile.

IT WAS A JOB
(my father's story)

We started work Saturday night,
after the last train had gone,
and worked all night, and around eight
the following morning
we went home and got changed
because it had rained all the time,
and then went back, and worked
all through Sunday. No choice,
you see, it was the 30s, and jobs
were few and far between, and they knew
that if we didn't work those hours
they could easily get others
who would be glad to.

I always remember that job
whenever I walk through the park,
and see that bridge over the river.
I was young then, and had steeplejacked,
so clinging to the side of a bridge
wasn't a problem, though the river
was high due to the rain.
I looked down a few times, and thought
what would happen if I fell.
They didn't care much about safety.
Still, it was a job, even if only
for a night and a day. Your mother
was glad of the money, I can tell you.

A GOOD DAY (2)

A good day is any day
when the surprising appears,
like a new book about Franz Kline,
or a Phil Urso record
you've wanted for forty years.

And you feel the thrill
that runs around your mind
("take your shoes off, baby")
and the sun is out, and things
will be perfectly fine,

while you sit and browse
through the book, and the black
and the white sing out,
just as you know the music will
when you get home later.

A good day is any day
when, as someone once said,
it's time to draw your water
from the nearest well,
and to sip at it slowly.

REFLECTION
        for Alan Dent

Suddenly reminded of the factory
where I worked for seven years,
I wonder why I stayed there all that time?
Hundreds of us every day,
clocking in and clocking out,
doing the same things, saying the same things.
It didn't make much sense then,
and it doesn't make any sense now.
Puzzled, I sit like an old Chinese poet,
and reflect on the foolishness of my life.

SMALL TOWN BOYS

Driving through Ohio with friends,
and we detour to Garrettsville.
Small town America, with its main streets,
gas stations, Edward Hopper store-fronts.
The sun burns down, and I'm taken
to see a plaque outside a building.
Hart Crane was born here, it says,
and I want to imagine him on Saturday night,
desperately trying to find a sailor,
hunting for an elusive drink,
and asking the farm boys what they think
of his new poem about his grandmother's letters.
The quiet town gives me no sign,
but a few days later, in New York,
I stand below the Brooklyn Bridge,
then go up Times Square to Columbus Circle,
and when I do, I hear the lines
that made their mark on me
in the mean streets of small town England
as I watched the curtain lift despite it all.

ARIA

My mother always loved opera,
not that she ever got to see one,
and when a singer trilled high notes
from the old radio in our house
she would pause and smile to herself.

I remember those moments.
The gloom of the small kitchen,
the smell of food cooking,
the hands wiped across the apron.
The peaceful look on her tired face.

REFLECTIONS OF AN OLD CHINA HAND

Waiting for a visit from an old friend.
I sit writing poems in the fading light.
Another day has come and gone,
and I'm no wiser. The old ideas
seem harder to sustain, the world we knew
is changing too fast for our comfort.
No-one believes what we believed,
hardly anyone understands what it meant.
I think of the years that have passed,
and look forward to the wine we'll share.

NATIONAL SERVICE

We were a nation of stoics.
Everyone we knew had served his time,
and a string of place names
would unravel when we met in the pub.
Germany, Suez, Korea, Malta, Cyprus,
Singapore, Hong Kong, and the rest.
Some had seen action, most not,
but it didn't matter, we had
the stupidity of sergeants,
and the mindlessness of mundane tasks
as factors we held in common.

"We did ours and you'll do yours,"
was a litany we chanted on Friday nights
as someone bemoaned his fate.
"Keep your noses clean," we said wisely,
"And never volunteer for anything."

We shrugged our shoulders
at some new example of bullshit,
and advised the victims to ignore it.
"What's the use of worrying?"
we asked, "It never was worthwhile."
We'd been there ourselves,
and knew what it was like.
We'd painted the brown grass green,
the coal white, and the grey stones red,
and it gave us a kind of comradeship,
a shared experience of a uniform life.

STATE EDUCATION

"What's the meaning of this?"
he would shout, bounding into the room,
and we would stop and stare,
and wonder what he was talking about.

We'd hazard guesses, and get clipped
around the head for our troubles.
But how were we to know his question
concerned our talking,

and that it wasn't meant to provoke us
into reflections on the nature of things?
How were we to know that he wasn't training us
for a role in future debates?

It was merely meant to silence us,
to put us firmly on the spot,
to let us know who was in control,
and to keep us in our lowly places.

Philosophy didn't come into it,
or maybe it did, and he didn't know it.
We'd sit, quiet under his baleful glare,
and think, "What's the meaning of this?"

ANOTHER NIGHT IN CHINATOWN

An ordinary night at the bus-stop
when the two T-shirted youths
wanted to know what was in my briefcase,
and had I any money on me.
"Books," I said, and "Not much,"
which is the way it usually is,
though they didn't believe me,
as they never do, of course,
and I began to back away from them.

Just then a group of noisy people
came out of a pub further down,
and the youths paused for a moment,
so I ran across the road and caught a bus
heading in the opposite direction.
"Better," I thought, "to be safe
going the wrong way than unsafe going right,"
smiling at my Chinese philosophy,
and smelling the fear from under my arms.

DEPARTMENT OF HUMAN RESOURCES

So, we were interviewing for these posts
of part-time seasonal workers,
and he said to one of the applicants
who was asking a lot of questions,
"Listen, do you want a job or not,
because if you don't want one on these terms
there are a hundred people out there
who will accept what we offer them."
And, of course, after we'd finished,
I said to him, you can't say things like that,
and he said, "But it's true, isn't it?"
so I replied, well, yes, it is,
but you're not supposed to say so.
He really isn't the type to have around
when you're picking and choosing who to hire.

EDEN REVISITED

Straining to knock a nail
into the wall, so she
could tie her rose bush to it,
I felt my feet slip off the chair.
A moment later, and I
was toppling backwards,
watching the world go upside down,
and waiting for the fall.

Dazed, I lay painfully
on the path, my spectacles
somewhere out of sight,
and heard her say, "You've broken
the chair." And I knew,
just at that moment,
what it was like in Eden
in between the good times.

ONE OF DE KOONING'S WOMEN

I went to see de Kooning's women
and ended up talking to the slim
blonde who didn't think much of
the work on the walls of the gallery
it isn't that I'm anti-art you
understand but it's the colours I
can't imagine a woman in that light
twisting her scarf to make the point
oh you know what I'm getting at
yes and I'm travelling back tomorrow
oh that's a pity I mean I'd love to
ok then we can walk down to Victoria
and get a tube from there it won't
take long and we'll have a few hours
her blonde hair merging into Easter
Monday and along the Embankment we
held hands and she said she didn't
know why she'd gone and one of her friends
had told her but isn't the river nice
the way the trees the bridge
we laughed at the girlie-magazines
in the window of the shop and she
said she couldn't see why men wanted
them like that and I shrugged and told
her how good she looked and when we
got to Leicester Square and the lights
were on and later walking along
Charing Cross Road she told me she was
leaving and when she turned to smile
with her blue eyes and blonde hair
it was like looking down a summer day
towards that point in the evening when
the birds stop singing and everything
is cool and still and starting to slide
into the dark pool of the night.

AND THE DEAD

And this is the room I sit in,
and this is the window I look out of
when I think about the dead.
And the dead come creeping in,
and stand staring over my shoulder,
and I hear their soft whispers,
and the room is cold and dark.

And outside the window the night
slides slowly over the rooftops,
and little lights dot the darkness,
like the lost signalling for help.
And this is the room I sit in,
and this is the window I look out of,
and the dead are many.

GROWING UP

Afternoons in shabby cinemas
as guns were pulled from holsters,
and bodies slumped
without a spot of blood in sight.
Evenings in the same seats,
while gangsters shot each other
with dramatic gestures,
and still without blood to be seen.
Saturdays and Sundays
when people fell from cliffs and castles,
died beneath trains and coaches,
or were cut to pieces by sharp swords,
though never with a hint of blood.
And then I saw a real person
die violently. A woman hit by a fast car.
She seemed to rise slowly in the air,
and come down, almost as in a film.
But there was blood everywhere.

110

BARBARIANS

My old Czech friend,
exiled in England,
would talk about Prague,
and the fact that he
would never go back
until the barbarians
had quit the place.
He meant the barbarians
from the East,
typified by the statue
of Joseph Stalin
overlooking the city.

Well, the barbarians
from the East
did eventually depart,
only to be replaced
by those from the West,
and a statue of a pop star
rose above Prague.
I think of my friend,
turning restlessly
in an English grave,
and dreaming of a time
when he can return.

THAT OLD FEELING

The usual musty smell,
almost unreadable spines,
and browned edges.
I pull some from the shelves,
and flick the dusty pages,
thinking about the lives
of those who wrote them.
Thousands of words
produced in expectation
of fame or immortality,
or maybe just money.
I see myself in years to come,
shabby and unread.

REGISTER NOW
"Funds may well be available from the
Arts Council as he is a registered poet"

There was a period
when poets dreamed about
participating in
some sort of revolution.
A few even desired
rented rooms in Paris
at weekly rates for all time.
But now they're happy to be
vetted by a committee.
No more Bohemia,
just Czechoslovakia in 1969,
where the bureaucrats
set the seal on behaviour,
and every poet is registered
or declared a non-poet;
where the right to inspiration
is limited
to those on a list.

THE COLD WAR

When he wouldn't name the names of those
who had fought with him in Spain,
they stopped his disability pension
from his service in the Second World War,
saying that he didn't deserve it,
and a true patriot wouldn't think twice
about informing on his friends.

When the old man who had been a sailor,
railroad worker, and union organiser,
was offered medical treatment in Moscow,
they refused him a passport
unless he could attend in person
at the Passport Office. His friends
had to take him there in an ambulance.

When the bureaucrats who made these decisions
retired on their comfortable pensions,
they settled in the country,
tending to their gardens,
and telling each other stories
about the good work they had done
to preserve the freedoms of the West.

THE LINE-UP
(one of my father's stories)

I'd hurry there first thing in the morning,
and I'd stand in line with the rest,
and the foreman would come along
with a pile of metal discs in his hand,
and walk down the line and look at us,
and he'd hand out a disc here and there
to a few familiar faces, or maybe on a whim,
and to anyone he knew would buy him drinks,
so that left thirty or forty of us
waiting to know if we would work that day,
and the foreman would pause and frown
and pretend he'd enough men for the job,
then throw the discs on the floor
and walk away smiling as men scrambled
and pushed and shoved for a chance
to take a little money home that night.

AGAINST THE TYRANNY OF MUSIC

The sounds are everywhere,
in pubs, shops, ships, restaurants,
aircraft, offices, factories.
You go to visit friends,
and they immediately sit you down,
and slip a CD into the machine.
The radio drills it at you all day,
the cinemas soften your mood
in every space between the films.

No-one needs to think with music
when it wallpapers the ears,
which is why it's so much easier
than reading books and magazines,
or looking at paintings.
People drift along in a daze,
not even noticing it
until it's turned off, and then
they stare in wild-eyed wonder.

It's silence, you say, and they
shuffle uneasily, and ask what time
the man will be down to repair
the cassette or the jukebox.
Silence, you whisper, and they shudder.
Silence, you mouth noiselessly,
and they begin to clap their hands
and mumble a tuneless chant
against a fear of the unknown.

THREE NOTES

1.

There is a moment, every now and then,
when I know what love is.
Like seeing you walk across
the departure lounge at the airport,
and realising with a warm feeling
that you're travelling with me.

2.

"I love cities," you said,
as we looked down on the roofs of Paris
from the heights of Montmartre.
Well, who wouldn't love cities
with hotel rooms in which
we can be close all night?

3.

The meal was good, the drinks also,
and your friend amusing.
We could have talked much longer,
but I wanted you to myself,
hungry for something more
than food, wine, and conversation.

POSING THE QUESTION

She used to send me photos,
taken by her husband, which showed her
lying naked on a bed,
or sitting astride a chair,
wearing only a belt and black stockings.

"He doesn't mind," she told me, "and says
it turns him on," and since then
I've never walked down a quiet street
without wondering what games
are played behind those neat curtains.

SPANISH LESSON

"You won't understand," he'd say,
"but bullfighting has grace and beauty.
You can't know this, coming from
the kinds of background that you do."

"What do you know about what happened
at five in the afternoon?
How can you appreciate the spectacle
of a brave man facing a brave bull?"

And he was always right, of course,
and we didn't know anything about it,
so we'd sit there, listening to him,
and taking in his barbed insults.

But when he closed in for the kill,
laughing at our crude mispronunciations,
we knew just how the bull felt,
and wanted to watch it gore the matador.

JUNE DAYS

And I sit in the Café le Rouquet
with Ted Joans and James Yates,
veteran of the Spanish Civil War.

I'm surrounded by history,
Bird flying high at the Open Door,
machine guns along the Ebro.

I see Hemingway across the road,
watch McAlmon order another drink.
Andre Breton looks down on us all.

I hear the last shot fired
by the last soldier of despair,
motor horns on the Boul. St Germain.

I sip cold beer, and listen
to them talking about George Whitman,
Shakespeare and Company.

And this is June in Paris,
where the streets are alive,
and everything seems possible.

MY MOTHER'S STORY

I visit my mother in hospital,
and listen to what she has to say.
Is that cat still here? she asks,
and tells me to look under the bed.

It followed me in last night,
and won't go away. A small, black cat,
not at all like Snowy,
the old white cat we once had.

Do you remember her? She used to wait
for my father to come home from the pit,
and she would run down the street,
and jump onto his shoulder.

He was a big man, over six feet tall,
and the neighbours, seeing Snowy
set against his grime, would shout,
"There's Matt Wilson and his cat."

Oh, she was a fine cat, Snowy was,
and he was a fine man, and didn't drink
like a lot of the miners did.
He died in 1915, killed in France.

I thought you were coming yesterday?
No, I reply, I said today,
and she says, That's strange,
and why did I think it was yesterday?

IRENE'S STORY

They brought the old lady in,
and she was raving. "They're coming,"
she said, "Don't let them get me,"
and we tried to soothe her, but she
just kept screaming and shouting.
"The Russians," she said, "The Russians."

"What's her background?" asked
the consultant, and someone said, "Oh,
she's German, born in Berlin.
She came here after the war," So I
held her in my arms, and kept saying,
"It's ok, you're with the British."

She calmed down then, and eventually
went to sleep, holding my hand,
and the consultant turned to
the junior doctors who'd expressed surprise
about the state the woman was in,
and how we'd managed to deal with her,

and he said, "Don't you people know
what happened to girls in Berlin in 1945?
Do you think you can understand people
when you don't know any history?
For God's sake, go to the library
and read something more than medical books."

NIGHT AND THE CITY

It is 10.30pm, a cold March night,
with a bitter wind
that takes the temperature below zero.
And there is a man
standing on the pavement,
not moving, not doing anything.
He is wearing a worn raincoat.
ill-fitting trousers, shoes so thin
they may as well not exist.

And I have been paid for reading poetry,
there is good red wine in my body,
I am heading for a comfortable house,
where I will sleep in a clean, warm bed.

As I pass the man he mutters,
and I understand that he wants money,
so I give him the change from my pocket.
I walk on, thinking of home,
but the man is still in the same place,
shoulders hunched against the night.
The wind works its way along the street,
and it cuts through the red wine,
and freezes the man in my mind.

POWER TO THE PEOPLE

And the people voted in a new government,
but it wasn't much different from the old one,
so nothing really happened,
except that down in the City something stirred,
and in Whitehall the mandarins
held more meetings, and thought of ways
to keep things as they were.
The poor were still poor,
and the rich were still rich,
the police still did what they had to do,
and the bureaucrats as little as possible,
while businessmen moved their money abroad,
and jobs continued to disappear,
until a few years later there was an election,
and the people voted in a new government.

POEM FOR ENTHUSIASTS

Give me the types
who are always enthusiastic,
who play their accordions
and let the decorating decline,
who frequent old bookshops
on rain-swept afternoons,
and sit in friendly pubs
reading crumbling paperbacks.
And those who write letters
to local newspapers to say
they collect travelling-irons,
and need a model 1329,
manufactured in Manchester in 1956,
and does anyone know
where one can be found.
Yes, give me people like that,
and spare me from meeting those
who talk of holidays and homes
and cars and careers,
but who never seem to know
where something rare lies hidden.

AN OLD LADY REMINISCES

When I was a little girl
my father took me to hear
Ben Tillet speaking.
He stood on a brewer's dray,
and all the people
gathered around him.
They were working people,
and you could see from the
expressions on their faces
that he was speaking for them,
and not to them,
with what he said about
how the future would be.

And on Saturday nights
my father's friends would come,
and they'd sit around
the kitchen table,
and drink their beer,
and talk about socialism,
books, and art and music.
I'd perch on my mother's knee
in the corner by the fire,
and listen to them.
My father wanted me to learn.
I often wonder what he'd say
if he knew how things are now.

BRIBERY AND CORRUPTION

Running the debt recovery section
in the local town hall,
I was always faced with the temptations
of the occasional favour or two.

A shopkeeper, behind with his rent,
would offer me free drinks
when I saw him in a nearby pub,
and he'd give me a friendly smile.

Another trader wanted to fill my freezer
with fresh fish, and one on the market
said I could have as much fruit
as I was able to carry away with me.

I only weakened once, though,
when I bought a couple of sausage rolls,
and the woman behind the counter
waved away my proffered five pound note.

"One good turn deserves another," she said,
meaning my leniency about her account.
I ate the rolls later, the flaky pastry
sticking uncomfortably in my throat.

TODAY THE STRUGGLE

They were huddled together in a corner,
seven or eight ageing men, gathered
to help the local Polytechnic launch its
documentary about the Spanish Civil War.
All around them academics, drinks in hand,
exchanged information about this prospect,
or that, the departmental gossip, the next
research grant or not, and where
to publish so that it will look good
when filling in application forms.
No-one paid much attention to the old men,
in their sober suits, until one of them,
swung across the room on his crutches,
a gap where a left leg should have been.
People let him through, and then
carried on with their brisk conversations.
The Spanish Civil War had come and gone.
The struggle today was what concerned them.

ART AND TECHNOLOGY

Are you surfing the Internet?
they ask, and I reply, "No,"
and they look at me as if I'm odd.
It is, they say, the only way
to go, technology is taking
us to new pastures.

I think of Lester Young,
his saxophone held together
with chewing gum and elastic bands,
creating beautiful music,
and slyly asking a technician
to sing him a song.

GOING HOME

Visiting my home-town
for the first time in a decade,
I see a procession
passing through the centre.

Festival week, someone says,
and I pause to observe
the floats and the pretty girls,
and the businesses cashing in.

Suddenly, a jazz band appears,
and I notice two old friends
strutting their paces in its ranks,
both bearded and bohemian still.

What keeps them going this way?
What makes them play
those bright and brassy sounds
as if they were fresh that day?

It's forty years or more
since I first heard them in a pub,
and they're just the same,
though age has thinned their hair.

Two elderly men whose lives
have been a part of my own,
laughing their way along the streets
of a shabby, industrial town.

HOW I'M DOING

Walking into the hospital, mid-afternoon,
feeling sorry for myself because of this
endless visiting, the dull hours saying little.

And I hear someone singing behind me,
"Powder your face with sunshine," he chants,
and louder, "Put on a great big smile,"

and I turn to see a legless man
handling his wheelchair at speed towards me.
"How are you doing, old son?" he shouts,

and I step aside as he laughs and passes by.
"How am I doing?" I wonder, aware that I'm on my feet.
and able to walk out when I'm ready.

THE BRIDGE

And there were those summer afternoons
when we would go down to the river,
and make our way along the path
that took us to the old bridge where,
the local people always reminded us,
the trams had once run into the country.

And we would swing out under the bridge,
high above the water, hand in hand
on the beams and iron stanchions
criss-crossing its underside, shouting
with joy and fear when a hand slipped
or a foot failed to connect properly.

And people would yell at us from above,
and from the river bank, calling us fools,
telling us to behave ourselves, saying
that they'd get the police if we didn't,
and all the time forgetting that they,
in their day, had done exactly the same.

And when we reached the other side,
we'd lie in the long grass beside the river,
listening to the water trickling over
the stones that we would have fallen onto
had we lost our hold, and then
we'd walk slowly back across the bridge.

LAYING SOMETHING DOWN

Sober and neat-suited, he stopped me
to ask if it was opening-time. I saw him
three days later, hungover and unshaven,
still in the same suit, now filthy.

"The best bricklayer in the town,"
someone said, "and he'd make a fortune
if he could only stay off the booze."

Years later, after he'd declined into
meths and anything else he could get,
he was beaten to death in a squalid room
where the local drunks gathered to argue.

And around the town are walls,
neat as that suit I once saw him in,
and still standing firm and straight.

FAMILY

I'd be out walking with my father,
and we'd pass a stranger, and my father
would nod at him, and I'd ask,
"Who was that, Dad?" and he'd reply.
"It was your Uncle Frank,"
and that was the end of the conversation.

Or sometimes, I'd see a chimney-sweep,
swaying slightly with his bike and brushes,
and he'd say, "You're Jimmy's boy,"
and I'd agree, and he'd press a coin
into my hand, and then ride off, drunkenly,
the soot drifting from his clothes.

And once I was taken to Liverpool,
and shown a large house where my father was born,
and told how the family business collapsed
due to my grandfather's drinking,
and his generosity to everyone in the pub.
"He boozed away a fortune," my mother said.

But I still don't know the full story
of how my father left home in the Twenties
when his family, good Catholics all,
told him to stop seeing my Baptist mother.
I just remember a stranger and a chimney-sweep,
and a father with very little to say.

WALKING THROUGH SOHO

Walking through Soho and I see
Paul Potts peering from a pub window.

Walking through Soho
and John Minton minces gaily by.

Walking through Soho and I hear
Colquhoun and MacBryde arguing in a doorway.

Walking through Soho
and W.S.Graham greets George Barker.

Walking through Soho and I turn
to enter David Archer's bookshop.

Walking through Soho
and Dylan Thomas lurches in front of me.

Walking through Soho and I know
I'll soon encounter Maclaren-Ross.

Walking through Soho
and Tambimuttu asks to borrow some money.

Walking through Soho and I think
about those who went before me.

Walking through Soho
where realities have become dreams.

WHAT I WANT

I want to die with Tippex on my fingers,
with the ink from changing ribbons
still staining my hands, while taking
a longing look at my typewriter
and seeing the bulldog clip that holds
parts of it together firmly in place.

I want to take a final breath
to tell a journalist who phones me
that he can't e-mail with questions,
nor send a fax, and why doesn't he
come to see me like a journalist should,
and, no, I don't have a mobile phone.

I want to see my last poems in a magazine,
and not on something called the Internet.
There is no replacement for paper.
And I want to get a letter from a publisher
saying they've received my typed manuscript,
and will bring out my posthumous poems.

SCARS

There is a faint scar
close to my right eye
and another
on the little finger
of my right hand.

Something that happened
as a child, though
I'm not sure what it was,
and I no longer
feel the need to know.

Like so many scars,
I carry them with me,
letting the reasons
slip into the past,
happy as they fade away.

CHRISTINE'S STORY

So he kept coming home drunk
and shouting for his dinner,
and I got so tired of it, you know,
that one day when he complained
and said the dog was treated
better than him, I emptied a can
of dog food into a pan and heated it up
and told him it was an Irish stew.
He ate it and went to sleep,
so I gave the dog the meat
I'd really bought for his meal.
Of course, I told him what I'd done
the next morning when he was hungover,
and he puked his heart out.
Served him right, the bastard.
He never shouted for his dinner again.

THE GRILL AND GRIDDLE

Not many of them left these days.
Plain furnishings, no radio or TV,
the table-tops easily wiped down.
The food, thick sausages, eggs,
tomatoes, crisp bacon, beans,
if you want them, and plenty of chips.
It attracts the locals who like it,
while the newcomers dress fashionably,
own large-wheeled cars, and drive miles
to fancier places for different food.

Saturday morning, and I talk about cats,
a neighbour's death, an accident
that blocked the street for an hour.
When I want to be left alone to read
the conversation carries on without me.
It's comfortable in a way
the modern can never be, and no-one cares
what you do as long as you're friendly
and don't disturb anyone else.

It's a good spot to be anonymous,
though an artist did once come to draw
what I suppose he thought were characters
from a time that's fading fast.
Was I the man at the back of the sketch,
his face hidden behind a newspaper?
He soon moved on, and things settled
into the usual routines of the everyday.
It's easy to be here, but don't ask me
where it is. We regulars like our lives
as they are, our pleasures undisturbed
by those who'd want to change everything.

HAPPY MAN BLUES

The old friend who dropped dead
in the street one day,
had played trombone all his life,
easing out sounds
in pubs and clubs and other places,
and never worrying too much
about how and when the money came in.

A bohemian existence? You could say that,
though he never would,
thinking it a pretentious term.
He just played his music,
drank a beer or two,
and smiled when he felt in his pocket,
and found very little there.

HARRY'S STORY

It was 1944 and I was in the army.
waiting to be sent overseas,
and I got a letter from my father,
asking, "Where's your wife?"
so I went to the CO and asked
for a few days leave so I could
go home and see what the problem was,
and when I got home the house
was locked up and she was gone,
and I never saw or heard from her again.
Not a thing, and no-one else
had any idea what had happened to her.
She'd just disappeared, completely,
without a word to anyone.
That was almost sixty years ago,
and I've been married twice since,
but I still wonder why she did it,
and where she went, and if
she's still alive somewhere.

DEMOCRACY

Today, I was stopped on the street
and asked for my opinion by a lady from the BBC.
And I thought of the scene in Viva Zapata!,
where someone explains to the peasants
that democracy is asking people for their opinions.
Suddenly, I felt moved to tears
by the fact that I had been engaged
in the democratic process. My opinion was valued.
Or at least I thought it was
until I listened to the radio programme,
and my voice was nowhere to be heard.

WORK

A neighbour tells me that her son
is about to embark on a period
of work experience, and I smile
and say that I first went to work
when I was sixteen, and it was
an experience I never did
get to enjoy. She looks at me
as if I'm odd, clearly thinking
I ought to be in favour of work
and the rewards it brings.
I reflect on my years working
and the hole in the sole of my shoe.

MISS TURNER

1943, and the war was nowhere near won.
In St Saviour's Infant School
we sat two to a small desk,
and learned our lessons by rote,
taught by elderly ladies brought back
to replace absent young men and women.

Miss Turner took a liking to me,
and some days would pull me to her,
and cradle my head between her breasts.
The war is now just a faint memory,
but thoughts of Miss Turner's ample bosom
still come easily to mind.

PERCY'S STORY

I was full of revolutionary fervour
when I was young, and in 1927
I decided to make a trip to Russia
to see how things were working out,
but I soon came back, disillusioned.
There were women wearing lipstick
and smoking in the streets.
Everyone said I was silly to say that,
but who's to say I wasn't right
when now you can see young girls
walking around dressed in a way
that would make the Marquis de Sade
think he'd entered Paradise?

KILLING CATS

When I was a child
I watched my father drown kittens
in an old bucket.
He held them under the water
until they stopped struggling.
The best thing for them, he said.

Around the same time
I helped a friend take a stray cat
to the local police station,
where they had a special gas oven.
A sergeant placed the cat inside.
They don't feel a thing, he said.

And not too long ago
I took our ageing ginger tom
to the local vet,
and held it down on the table
while he "put it to sleep."
It was the kindest thing, he said.

Now, at home, I stroke a new cat,
and she purrs in response
and eats the food I give her.
But she doesn't trust me too much,
and who can blame her?
I could kill her with kindness.

THE RIGHT PLACE AT THE RIGHT TIME

There was a man said he would die
in Paris on a rainy Thursday,
and I wonder how he knew that?

I don't know when I will die,
or where, and it doesn't worry me,
though occasionally I'm curious.

Paris on Thursday or any other day
would be fine by me. And London
on Friday might work just as well.

I'd hate to die in Preston on Sunday,
and Manchester on a damp Monday
has a sombre side I don't relish.

There are other places and other days,
and some sort of combination
is sure to resolve the problem.

Meanwhile, I take note of my location,
and the weather, and hope to survive
for another week or two.

THE DAY MY FATHER DIED

My father woke up one morning and died.
No-one asked him to, he just did it,
without fuss and with very few words,
which was the way he did most things.
"I don't feel well," he said,
and slid back into bed, where he lay,
a grimace on his face, or so my mother
told me when I saw her later that day.
"He had pains in his chest," she said,
"and I went downstairs to get some brandy,
and when I got back to the bedroom
it was too late and he was dead."
It was quiet in the street outside,
and beyond the window was a dark cloud.

THE QUESTION

Paddy, the Irish corporal,
would stagger into the room
two or three times a week,
open the window, climb onto the ledge,
and threaten to jump.
We were three storeys up,
in an old German army barracks,
so we'd leap out of bed,
drag him back, and spend
an hour or so reassuring him
that life really was worth living.

But he did it once too often,
and no-one moved, and a voice said,
"So jump you stupid bastard,
and then we can get some sleep."
He climbed back, closed the window,
and went quietly to bed.
That was almost fifty years ago,
but I still think about that night,
and what would have happened
had he disappeared into the dark.
Would I now sleep easy?

WORK EXPERIENCE

I am reading an article
by a lady from the Institute of Directors,
in which she assures the readers
that we are all employees now,
and there is no such thing as "Them and Us."

And my mind goes back fifty years,
to the day I first started work in a cotton mill,
and seeing a person in a suit
who seemed quite pleasant,
I remarked on his good nature,
to which an old man standing nearby said,
"Son, he's a boss, and a boss is a boss,
and they're all bastards."

And it occurs to me that,
despite what the lady from the Institute says,
nothing much has happened in my life
to make me think that the old man
was wrong in what he said.

GESTURES

There's not much you can do anymore,
apart from make a few gestures.
You can make them from barricades,
and with crosses on pieces of paper,
though they're not really any use.
You can make them up against a wall,
if that is to your liking,
or you can make them with poems,
and music, and painting.
The trouble with gestures like those
is that they're more than likely
to get turned into things
against which gestures have to be made.
You can make gestures against gestures,
and it's probably right to do so,
provided you never forget
that is all you are doing.
Finally, you should know that you
are always allowed a final gesture.
Permanent silence is the favourite one.

A SMALL MEMORY

I have this memory
of my grandmother,
a small woman in a small house
not too far from the harbour
of a small northern seaport.
You could hear the gulls
and smell the fish
when you opened the window
in the morning,
and downstairs in the kitchen
there would be fresh bread
and tea, and sometimes an egg.
She was always busy,
and I'd go into the street
to keep out of her way
while she got her work done.
The neighbours would ask me
how long I was staying this time,
and I'd tell them, and run off,
down to where the fishing fleet
was leaving the harbour.
I'd wave wildly at small figures
moving around the decks
of scruffy trawlers,
then they'd be small dots
almost on the horizon,
and I'd walk back to that
small house, and the small woman
busy preparing good food,
and she'd ask what I'd done,
and I'd tell her and she'd nod,
then carry on
with her numerous small tasks.

THINGS

"We're sorting out her things,"
my sister tells me over the phone,
"Is there anything you want?"

"No, " I say to her, thinking that
I have what I want in my mind,
a portrait of someone small,

who, over the years, taught me
that beauty is all around us,
and "things" don't matter at all.

SPRING IN PARIS

I saw him walking along the rue Rambuteau,
and he clutched his bottle of cheap wine
as if there wouldn't be another that day.
Crowds of tourists went by but he didn't beg,
he had his wine, enough for the time ahead,
and what he would do when it was gone
was something to be worried about later.
There was sufficient for the moment.
And just then, despite everything I knew,
and with my progress carefully planned,
I wanted to be like him, not measuring hours,
and simply concerned to catch that feeling
when a sip of wine is all that is needed
to satisfy the desire for something more.

LOVE POEM

I am reading James Sallis,
and listening to Sarah Vaughan,
alone in my room.
Well, not quite alone,
the cat is stretched
by the fire, his forepaws
folded in front of his breast.

The book is entertaining,
the music is charming,
as only old music can be,
the cat a pleasure to look at.
I ask myself what more
do I want, and wait
for your knock at the door.

STRANGER IN A STRANGE LAND

If there's one thing that bores me,
it's football, and this man on the train
is trying to involve me in a conversation
about some player or another
I've absolutely no interest in.
"But don't you think," he says,
that he should be in the team?"
I shrug, and he pauses, and asks,
"Don't you want to talk?"
and I reply, "Not about football,"
and he looks surprised, and says,
"Well, which planet are you from?"

HELMUT'S STORY

So, we went down to the village
and got four Frenchman and shot them.
And what would you have done?
We'd been there two years,
and they'd worked with us,
taken our money in their shops and bars,
and we'd had no problems at all,
and then, one night, two of our boys,
and that's all they really were,
were shot in the back as they walked
along a country road, unarmed.
It wasn't as if the war was near us,
or we'd done anything to them,
and most of us never wanted to be there,
we were conscripts, just like you,
and look what happened the other week
when one of your comrades was hurt
in a fight in the town, and a crowd
of your soldiers went down there
and they really wrecked that pub.
So, I ask you, what would you have done
if you had been with me in France?

THE PULL OF DANGER

Church Deeps, they called it,
the part of the river below the church
where you weren't supposed to swim
because of undercurrents and whirlpools
and stories of missing people.

Of course, we did swim out there,
feeling the cool flow of the water,
hearing the shouts of warning
from the far bank, and waiting
for that first pure pull of danger.

ROUGH JUSTICE

The lieutenant was a bully
and one private, in particular,
bore the brunt of his bad temper,
picked up for untidiness on parade,
booked for incorrect equipment
during a routine inspection,
and denied permission to leave camp
because he was, the lieutenant said,
in need of a haircut. The private
spent most of his time doing
extra guard duties or parading
in full kit several times a day.

It went on and one day, returning
to camp after a couple of weeks leave,
the private was told by the lieutenant
that he was on a charge for being late.
That night, the private somehow
got hold of a rifle and ammunition
and waited for the lieutenant,
who told him he hadn't the guts to pull
the trigger. "You don't need guts,
you need a finger," the private said,
and shot the lieutenant. None of us
bothered to mourn his passing.

DESIRE

She said there was a Princess in Italy
who could make men quiver with desire
simply by peeling off one of her gloves,
and I thought, yes, that's fascinating.

I'd been at an exhibition earlier that day,
paintings of ladies in long dresses
with high necklines, and I could imagine
how a glimpse of a wrist would be exciting.

And later, walking through the streets,
passing women wearing very little,
I began to see how much I was missing
by being shown almost everything.

THE TRAVELLER

He liked to drink in airports
and in bars at railway-stations.
Not that he ever wanted to go anywhere,
other than to get to where he was.
But he liked the atmosphere of places
where people came and went,
and the fact that no-one knew him.
He could remember a friend of his
who always said that it was time
to stop visiting a pub
when the landlord asked your name.

He would sit in the bar, relaxing,
and he'd sip his drink slowly
and listen to the announcements.
People occasionally talked to him,
saying where they were going and why,
and they usually looked surprised
when he said he wasn't travelling,
and more surprised when he told them
he didn't want to go anywhere.
That was the moment he liked best,
the puzzled looks on their anxious faces.

PERE LACHAISE

Paris again, and I visit Pere Lachaise
and stand before Le Mur des Federes,
thinking about the Rue Ramponeau
and that afternoon in May
when the last barricade was abandoned.

Behind me, packed closely together,
are gravestones and monuments
to Resistance fighters and veterans
of the Spanish Civil War, and Jews
who were rounded up and slaughtered.

It's a dull Sunday morning, and a couple
stop to ask me if I know where
they can find the grave of someone famous.
I point into the distance, and a
thin rain begins to fall on the forgotten.

DOMESTIC SCENE

He is talking to her, and she
is examining her fingers.
"Oh, look," she says, "this one
is longer than the other hand,
let me check it against yours."
He is surprised, and wonders
what her hands have to do
with existential theory
and American films of the Forties.

"There's this scene," he says,
"where the woman wants to kill someone,
and is wondering how to do it."
He pauses, and looks at her
as she continues to hold up
both her hands thoughtfully.
"I don't think you listen to me,"
he complains, and she says, softly,
"No, but I hear you all the time."

PEACE IN OUR TIME

The pub around the corner
was called The Sebastopol,
on Inkerman Street, which had
Balaclava Road and Alma Crescent
running off it. And the
monument in the park
had names like Ladysmith
and Spion Kop
carved into its stone.

During the day, my father
a veteran of the Great War,
worked in a factory,
constructing bombers,
and my mother made munitions.
Meanwhile, I was looked after
by an old lady whose thoughts
still hovered around sons
killed on the Somme.

And in the streets,
we regularly pulled the triggers
that wiped out our enemies
from the houses across the road.

LISTEN TO THE STORIES

So, imagine the scene,
a bar frequented by musicians,
somewhere in New York,
and in walks Charlie Parker.
He goes to the jukebox,
inserts a couple of coins,
and then heads for a drink
as the music starts to play.
Country and Western: sad songs
of lost dreams, broken hopes,
midnight trains, and even
a happy time or two.

When the music stops,
Parker goes again to the jukebox,
and, again, chooses to play
some Country and Western sounds.
After the third selection
a well-known jazz trombonist
turns to him, and asks,
"Hell, Bird, what is it
with all this corny stuff?"
And Parker looks at him,
and says, with a little smile,
"Listen to the stories, man."

HISTORY

I used to see her going to the shops,
a small figure in a frayed coat.
Just another of the pensioners
from the bungalows on the estate.
A retired nurse, someone told me,
and she never has much to say.

Years later, I heard she'd met Stalin
when she was in Russia in the Twenties,
had nursed wounded in the Spanish Civil War,
and survived the Blitz in London.
Oh yes, tell me all about history,
and the famous people who made it.

RELIGION

She was telling me about how,
when she was a little girl,
she'd watch the Whit Walks,
Catholics on one day, Protestants
on another, and if it was fine
when the Catholics walked,
but rained on the Protestants,
her mother would smile, and say,
"God surely knows his own."

And I thought of Beziers
during the Albigensian Crusade,
with 200 Cathars among the
total population of 8,000,
and when the Crusaders broke in
their commander wondered how
to tell the Cathars from the others.
"Kill them all," he was told,
"God will know his own."

LITERARY TALK

"There are a few mistakes
in your book," she said,
and I said, "There have been
a few more in my life."

"Still," she said, "you can
correct them in the next edition,"
and I laughed, and said,
"Do you think there'll be one?"